Live Tax Free Forever

(through Your Solo 401K)

Michael J. McDermott, SDA

ISBN:1468002015
ISBN-13: 978-1468002010

DEDICATION

There are so many that it is hard to pick one. My siblings, Peg, Joe and Pat. The Kneelands. Steve Schaaf. Rick Heaton. Jodi Amerell. Monica Forgues and the caregivers. But especially to Linda for her forbearance, love and support without which none of this is possible.

CONTENTS

ACKNOWLEDGMENTS

Special thanks to David Marca whose encouragement , dedication and experience brought this book to bear.

An unpayable debt of gratitude to Joshua Sharp whose knowledge permeates these chapters.

Kudos to Isabel for the great art work on the cover.

1. Every Party Needs a Pooper
(that's why we invited them)

Much has been written about, and many websites exist touting the "Tax Havens" around the world. Establish off-shore accounts to avoid taxes and legal action, they tell you. Get a Swiss bank account, open an account in the Caiman Islands. Become divorce, legal action and tax proof. They all beg the question of residency. Put simply, you may not live, dwell, or exist in the United States while taking advantage of these tax havens. Oh, don't get me wrong. You can live here and establish them there, but when push comes to shove, and you're expecting to really take advantage of them, you may find them less than useful.

> **Judge** – Mr. Dodge, it has come to our attention that you have accounts off shore. Please bring that money back to the US and make it available to this plaintiff.
>
> **You** – Sorry your honor, you can't make me do that.
>
> **Judge** – Bailiff, take Mr. Dodge to jail on contempt of court. I order that he be detained until that money shows up in our little hands.

Yes, it's true. The court CAN'T make you bring the money back to the US, but they can hold you in contempt until you do.

Bear in mind, I'm writing this for the average US Citizen, not your typical drug lord, extortionist, or embezzler. If you generate legal income, it's difficult to bury, hide or otherwise conceal "legal" money. If you want to do that using off-shore accounts, you'll have to take your body off-shore as well. It's hard for a judge to court-order anything regarding you if you live in the Azores. But you can establish tax free accounts right here in the United States using the same tools that have been available to everyone since 2006.

Our tax codes are established to accomplish two things besides the obvious of getting money for the government: 1.) They're designed to incent people to perform certain actions and 2.) They're designed to punish people who don't take those actions. WAIT! Did I say punish? Yes, I did. Imagine sending your child to a birthday party. Your little party-goer shows up with the required present, full of anticipation for a great time. The host of the party sits your little loved one on a hard chair where all the merriment and fun can be witnessed, and when the other kids are served pizza, soda, cake and ice cream, your child is given a baloney sandwich and a glass of milk. Now mind you, the love of your life was cared for, and possibly the baloney sandwich and milk were more nutritious than the fat and sugar present in the pizza, cake and ice cream. So can we say this is punishment?

YES! Of course we can. Your child would never want to go back and you yourself would never allow attendance there again. Yet this is exactly how our tax code works. On the one hand, there is a hard chair reserved for you with your name on it. Our tax code invites you to sit and squirm. On the other hand, there is a HUGE party buried in our tax code. If you're a kid, the tax code is all cake and ice cream, if you're a bachelor, it's a bachelor party, if you're a mom, it's a Tupperware party with all your best friends. In short, it's the best party you can imagine. And the cool thing is, you're all invited. It's just that your invitation got lost in the mail.

But it's an on-going party being thrown by our mutual uncle – Uncle Sam. Furthermore, it's being thrown on an island that is completely tax free. There actually are multiple islands you can pick from. They exist in Wisconsin, Illinois, Iowa, Minnesota, Alaska, Pennsylvania, Arizona, Utah, Colorado, Wyoming, Nebraska, Texas, Oklahoma, Missouri, and every other state in the union. You don't have to fly there, boat there, or make any travel arrangements. You can get there in the comfort of your own home and in your own car. You'll need a phone, some training, and some good advice (the proper attorney, accountant, real estate agent, and a few other professionals). You'll need a little imagination and some determination, but with a little help, you'll be able to exercise your invitation and live the rest of your life on Party Island. You see, Party Island doesn't exist as a real place. It only exists in our current tax code.

Oh, and you have to bring friends.

Points to Remember

1. It's time to reframe your thinking.
2. The tax code is designed to reward you.
3. The tax code rewards entrepreneurs.
4. The tax code will allow you to live tax free.
5. Living well and enjoyably is up to you.
6. Your most valuable asset is your attitude. Guard it well.

2. The Party's Over (So They Say)

There are fundamentally two types of complainers – Hand Wringers and Fist Shakers. These are people to be avoided in your life and throughout the implementation of the ideas brought forth in this book. These are people that will suck the life out of your dreams and the wind out of your sails. No matter what you try to accomplish, these folks will tell you how and why your plan won't work and exactly what is wrong with it, what's wrong with "the system" as well as what's wrong with the world that will prevent you from reaching your goals.

Since we're focused on your financial future, there are two groups that I want to steer you away from. These people expound their opinions, which are usually unfounded, or worse, founded on someone else's unfounded opinions, and always their view is this: "You have no control, the "system" works against you, and you can't win."

Even if they don't say it directly, that's the overall message hidden in their rantings. As you read this, you may recognize some of these people. If you do, you'll know from now on to keep your conversations limited to non-essential topics, that is, non-essential to your financial freedom. Worse though, you may actually recognize yourself in these people. You may find that you have expounded on these topics in the past, and you may have promoted some of these thoughts yourself. If that is the case, I urge you to do one of two things: 1.) Understand that your attitudes, though difficult to change, can be amended to something more positive. You can adopt an "I can take control" attitude. Or 2.) Put this book back on the shelf, give it back to the person who gave it to you, sell it to Half Price Books or on Amazon, or donate it to Goodwill. I'm assuming that you will fall into the first category and continue reading. If you can make it through the first chapter, you will qualify to continue to free yourself from worry, drudgery, and most of all, taxes.

Hand wringers and fist shakers complain about a variety of things wrong with the world, but the two I want to address are these: The Gold Standard and the IRS. I want to address these because they directly affect what you will be trying to accomplish. Both of these relate to your finances, but more directly they relate to your attitude about your finances. I cannot stress enough, your money, your wealth and your financial position have very little to do with the number of green slips of paper you possess or of some number on an account statement, but have everything to do with your attitude and beliefs. Let's tackle some of these beliefs right now.

The Gold Standard

"Oh, our economy is all messed up!" or "Our money is controlled by a private corporation, not even the government." or "We'd be doing a lot better on the gold standard." People will waste a lot of your time and mental resources trying to convince you that this is true. Admittedly part of this is true: our economy is all messed up. But guess what! Our economy has always been "all messed up." We've been on the gold standard and off the gold standard a number of times, and the economy was still always all messed up. As a matter of fact, there were times we went off the gold standard to un-mess it. Abraham Lincoln took us off the gold standard during the civil war. Franklin D. Roosevelt took us off the standard for the most part during the depression and Richard Nixon drove the last nail in the coffin So now we have a "FIAT" currency. That isn't a currency based on an Italian car manufacturer; rather it's currency that's accepted as valuable because the government declares it so.

As much as our hand wringers and fist shakers espouse the benefits of the gold standard, we can pretty much assume that the gold standard is dead. It was dying slow death in the 1930s and Nixon shocked it to death on August 15th, 1970. More than a cursory glance at history will show that there were numerous panics and recessions in the 1800s that, if not caused by the gold standard, certainly weren't prevented by it. The worldwide depression in the 20th century exemplifies this. Those countries that clung to the gold standard the longest suffered from the depression the longest.

Let's look at the gold standard for a second. That's really about all it deserves. I want you to get out twenty pennies and put them on the table or desk in front of you. Let's imagine that these pennies represent all the currency issued in our gold backed system and each penny has the same amount of gold in Fort Knox. Get out a pen, a pencil, an eraser and a piece of paper. GREAT! Now imagine that those four items represent the total output of our society, that is, all the production we can have in one year. Nice and even, right? Good so far. Now take another piece of paper and add it to the mix. This represents the increase in production that we need to sustain growth in our economy. Well, let's see what happens. We had four commodities to begin with each going for five cents. But now with the increase, we have 5 commodities and the maximum they can be worth is four cents. Now add a pencil. Oops, 6 items and only 20 cents. That doesn't work out evenly. Add an eraser. It's just getting worse. Can't we print more money to represent the increase in production? Yes, but it no longer represents the amount of gold we have. We still only have 20 units in Fort Knox, so we need to maintain twenty pennies and no more.

Now add all the pencils in your drawer, all the pens that have accumulated in your desk, the ream of paper you took your first two sheets from, all the erasers in your kids' bedroom or book bag, and you can see that the twenty cents doesn't go very far in trading those commodities. The monetary system can no longer represent the value of the economy.

As confusing, baffling and complicated as it seems, today's monetary system attempts to represent the production of the country, rather than some arbitrary amount of some arbitrarily chosen metal. How well does it do that? The gold standard people seem to think it doesn't do it well at all, and the economists seem to think that it fails and succeeds in varying degrees at various times. But it works better than the gold standard. Our economy in the US is so vast now that there is not enough gold in the world to represent it, much less represent the economies of all the foreign countries as well. Maybe if we came up with the gold, silver, platinum, palladium, iridium, osmium, uranium, cesium, mercury, molybdenum, etc. standard, we could have metals approximate our economic system, but that will never happen either. We'd run out of elements there too.

To make matters more confusing, today's electronic transactions actually create money. A system such as a gold standard which limits the printing of money based on chunks of metal held in a vault wouldn't allow for the growth of our financial markets, issuing of loans, or increased production of real goods.

One final example: I found a pay stub of my father's from 1933. He was a lineman for the Interstate Power Company. He worked 114 hours in two weeks. His take home pay was $37.50 which means he earned between 33¢ and 34¢ per hour. If we were on the gold standard, and had absolute parity with the standard in 1933, a $60,000 per year occupation would still pay about $1,000.00 per year.

In reality even the gold standard is a fiat standard. Gold is only valuable because everyone agrees it is.

So the long and the short of this diatribe is that our fiat system is the system of currency we have. You can shake your fist and declare it doesn't work, or you can wring your hands and worry that it doesn't work, but when you're all done, take a deep breath, look around and try to determine what system of currency we have. If we still have the fiat system, shake and wring some more. If shaking and wringing makes a difference in your life, if you become more empowered by shaking and wringing, keep doing it. Please donate this book to your local charity immediately.

One concession we can make to the gold standard people is that our money is fundamentally worthless. Think about this. Absorb it, understand it. In truth, ALL money is fundamentally worthless. Little slips of green paper (now orangish and purple too) are worth anything only because you and I and a bunch of other people agree it is. Money grows less valuable with time due to inflation. So wealth cannot be gained by getting more money.

This is very important to understand. You cannot become wealthy by getting more money.

So why all this talk about the gold standard? First, you need to have confidence in what you are going to do. As messy as our monetary system is, it's still better than the gold standard. Is our dollar strong? Is it weak? Is it going to collapse tomorrow? It doesn't matter! You have a fundamental set of tools to work with and part of those tools is the economic system we have. We don't have any other. So rather than spend your valuable resources, that is, your emotional and mental capital on frivolous arguments, turn your attention to something that will enrich you: something like our tax code.

The Truth about Our Tax Code

Yes, our wringers and shakers love to decry our tax code. “Flat tax! Flat tax!” we hear them shout. The flat tax would be more fair! The flat tax would be easier! The flat tax would simplify our lives!

It would be wonderful if we all got to pay a flat tax. Look on the form, see the percentage, everyone pay. Unfortunately our system doesn’t work that way, and whether we like it or not, the gigantic aircraft carrier of our tax system is plowing its way forward through the ocean of our economy. I’m using the aircraft analogy for one simple reason. There are no brakes on a ship like that. The inertia of our system carries it forward, but beyond that is the long tradition of our legislators and the political system as a whole to use our tax code as an incentive to get the populous to act a certain way. When the government wants us to perform a certain behavior, the congress and the president pass laws that become incorporated into the tax code that reward people by reducing or eliminating taxes for certain investments. When actions or investments are deemed detrimental to the health of the nation, particularly the financial health, tax credits and deductions disappear, or worse, taxes are imposed.

A great example of this is the Tax Reform Act of 1986. Prior to ’86, our tax code was extremely complex (as though it isn’t now!), favoring those who took the time to understand and exploit it. Furthermore, certain investments could generate passive deductions that people could use against ordinary income. Ordinary income includes wages, tips, commissions, salaries and income from businesses in which you are materially involved (in most senses, WORK). Think W-2s and 1099s, although there are variations. Now PASSIVE deductions come from investments that generate income and losses that don't involve active participation. Most people would relate to rental properties. The rent is passive income and the depreciation of the building would represent a passive loss. An entire financial industry arose out of designing investments called Limited Partnerships that would allow an investor, particularly one with high income, to garner passive losses that could offset his active income. One could invest in real estate deals, oil exploration, cattle, horses, movies and any number of vehicles that would allow one to reduce the amount of tax paid, while earning some nominal amount on the investment. These investments were seen as detrimental to the overall health of our economy, so the Tax Reform Act of 1986 eliminated passive deductions (well, almost eliminated) for people (well, most people) who wanted to use them against ordinary income. Limited Partnerships fairly well disappeared from the investment scene. The good news for the smart investor is that these deductions still exist and are quite easy to come by if one knows how. It's one of the benefits of being at the party.

And there is a heck of a party going on. If you are a W-2 wage earner, you are sitting on a hard chair, drinking plain white milk, eating baloney sandwiches while other people are eating cake and ice cream, playing pin the tail on the donkey, and having the time of their lives. The tax code smiles very favorably on business owners, investors, and especially the real estate industry. For most people who collect their paycheck, put it in the bank, then wonder where to get extra money, our tax code tolerates them. It gives them very little lee way to nudge the income they need to get into a higher tax bracket, into a better way of life. But for the group of knowledgeable individuals, the party still rages.

Please Please Please, Learn to Love Our Tax System!

You've seen them and you get emails from them. They rant and rave. They scream of impending doom. They tell us the Federal Reserve isn't a branch of the government, it's a private corporation that's run by an international illuminati that are ready and waiting to pull the gold fillings from your grandchildren's teeth. They swear that big government is in cahoots with big business, the banking system runs Congress and Wall Street runs everything else.

Okay, so what if it's true? Write your Congressman? Run for office? Hide gold under the foundation of your house? Buy guns and freeze dried peas? The prophets of doom have always used fear and uncertainty to compel people who are easily led to hunker down and stop using the tools they've been given for a happier, healthier life and to invest in their cockamamie schemes.

If you're responding right now that "'So and so' predicted the crash of the eighties, and he was right," then this is not the book for you. This is the book for people who understand there are a vast number of tools at their disposal that, when implemented properly, will provide them with the safety, the security, the knowledge and the comfort supplied by true wealth.

What is True Wealth?

First, wealth is NOT money. Money is a slip of paper or a chunk of metal that a bunch of people agree is worth a certain number of goods and services. I don't care if it's gold, platinum, Einsteinium, or anything else.

If you can't get people to agree that whatever you're offering is worth something, it's worthless. Take a 3 oz gold bar into a restaurant some night and try to get seated, or better yet, once you've eaten, offer it in payment (as of the writing of this book, that would be approximately $3,672.00). You can see that regardless of the value of your offer, if the people you're offering it to don't want it, then it's pretty much worthless.

As a general rule, money becomes less valuable over time. Our system feeds on inflation, and moderate amounts of inflation are considered good. Our system never thrives on deflation. Deflationary periods are serious and cause suffering at all economic levels. Even though they occur, deflationary periods never counteract the cumulative effect of inflation. Hence, our money grows cheaper by the day. If all you have is money, you have a depreciating asset.

So what is true wealth? Think about your life. Everything you touch, taste, smell, wear, drive, write on, write with, email over, and anything else you can think of, comes out of the ground. Oil becomes fuel, plastic, fabric and comes out of the ground. The concrete, brick and mortar of your house, along with any wood comes out of the ground. The fabric in the clothes you wear comes out of the ground, or possibly off a sheep which grows because of the stuff it eats which comes out of the ground. Any means of production is built on some ground. So the long and short of it is, true wealth comes out of the ground. If I were going to amass true wealth, I would certainly begin checking out the ground, and discovering how to go about owning some of it.

So I can definitely say that a real estate investor is well grounded. Or perhaps, a well grounded investor owns real estate. This becomes obvious when you understand two facts:

1. The majority of individuals in the United States who have become millionaires have done so in real estate.
2. The business that receives the most deductions under the IRS tax code is real estate.

Now please don't get me wrong. I'm not encouraging you to run out to get your real estate agent's license. Nor do I want you to get your broker's license. If you haven't already started, then I want you to consider investing in real estate. And I want you to consider investing in real estate within your retirement plans. When you consider all the advantages of owning real estate, owning property in a retirement plan is like holding a magnifying glass over it. The benefits of real property enhance the power of the plan, and the power of the plan amplifies the benefits of real estate.

Bear in mind, this book focuses on real estate as the main alternative investment to consider. There are, however, limitless investments available to you as a savvy or even not so savvy investor. Did you know you could buy truckloads of hay in Nebraska and ship them to Texas in your IRA? Buy and sell cattle? Own part of Danicka Patrick's race car? Ship containers of hardwood from Brazil to Germany? Produce movies?

In short, you can invest in anything where you might have experience and proficiency. You no longer have to be shackled to Wall Street, mutual funds, annuities and bank accounts. Understanding the basics of your retirement plan is the key to removing your handcuffs. Putting them into practice not only unshackles you, but allows you to host your own party.

When you finish this book, you should be able to

1. Understand the differences of the various tax advantaged accounts.

2. Understand the implications of taxes, when they are incurred and their affects on your return and your future.
3. Compare the various plans to judge their advantages to you in various situations.
4. Accurately judge what investments are best for you, and how to use them for your retirement.
5. Plan for early withdrawals from your retirement plans to allow you to prosper at a younger age.
6. Live income tax free at a desired point in your life.

You will have the basics that will allow you to enjoy your efforts immediately as well as in some distant future. You will be able to protect your estate with tax free dollars as well as saving tax free dollars. You will be able to buy your ideal retirement vacation home with tax free dollars and ultimately you will give your kids, your grandkids and any charity or foundation you choose a legacy they can't outgrow or outspend.

Oh, and did I mention that you will be able to benefit any community in which you do business, structuring win-win deals for all involved? Did you know you can thrive doing good while you're doing well? Did you realize that you can profit by helping others profit from this knowledge? And did you know that while the media and the majority of the advisors out there are screaming "sky is falling" messages, that NOW is the perfect time to use the strategies in this book to control your future?

The seal on the back of the book says "Ego Imperium", which means "Self Control". This book is dedicated to those of you who want to control your finances, your future and your lives.

Points to Remember

1. Don't waste your mental resources on non-essentials.
2. We might hate taxes, but we love our tax code.
3. Real estate offers access to true wealth.
4. The majority of people in the US who have become millionaires have done so in real estate.
5. The greatest number of tax breaks are given to real estate professionals.
6. You can control your own life and retirement.

3. Knowledge Is NOT Power

We've heard it forever: Knowledge is power. This was usually told to us by teachers that had to impress upon us, especially as freshmen in high school, that algebra was not a complete waste of time. They were wrong. (About knowledge, not algebra.)

Knowledge is FREEDOM!

Action is POWER!!!

The more knowledge you have, the more freedom you have. It's very simple. The ability to make informed decisions makes for more freedom in your life. But knowledge without action is dead. Imagine a library at a university that contains all the knowledge on all subjects in the world. The knowledge is there, but none of those books are going to design a rocket to ship men into space. They won't perform microsurgery on a tiny nerve center in your brain, giving you back your life. They won't raise a child, bait a fishhook, cook a gourmet meal or thaw a frozen pipe. It's all dead knowledge.

Conversely, action without knowledge is fruitless, even detrimental. As one wise man said "Action without thought is like shooting without aim." Imagine the mindless action of a crowd rioting. Remember the actions of a child throwing a tantrum. How about a car careening out of control? This chapter dedicates itself to checking your knowledge. The following is a brief test to gauge yourself and your perceptions of retirement plans.

The "Quick, What Do You Know about Retirement Plans?" Quiz

1. I bought an IRA and it lost money. T F

2. I bought an IRA and it made money. T F

3. An IRA is:
   a. A tax free investment
   b. A Gershwin brother
   c. A tax structure in the IRS code
   d. b & c

4. A Self Directed Retirement Plan can only be established by:
   a. Anyone with income
   b. Anyone with earned income
   c. A qualified institution like a bank or brokerage firm
   d. Anyone between ages 18 -70 ½

5. It is possible to get your money out of an IRA before retirement without penalty. T F

6. Combining retirement plans for investments is strictly illegal. T F

7. Commingling Roth and Traditional IRAs is strictly illegal. T F

8. I can pull money out of my retirement plan for investment purposes. T F

9. What can be purchased by self directed IRAs?
   a. Only mutual funds
   b. Any investment through a broker, bank or insurance company

c. Just about anything including collectibles, S-Corps and life insurance
d. Just about anything excluding collectibles, S-Corps and insurance

10. My brother-in-law loves pizza, so he wants his retirement plan to purchase and run a pizza parlor. Of course he can't do this. T F

11. The age limits for contributing to a Roth IRA are:
a. 18 at the youngest, 70 ½ at the oldest
b. 21 at the youngest, 59 ½ at the oldest
c. Newborn to Methuselah – no limit
d. 18 at the youngest, 59 ½ at the oldest

That wasn't so bad, was it?

Answer Key

1. No you didn't.
2. No you didn't. (The answers to number one and number two are contained in question #3.)
3. The correct answer is D. b and c. George Gershwin was the composer, Ira was the lyricist. (Ok, it's a silly joke, so if you had C. that's acceptable too.) But an IRA is nothing more than a provision in the IRS code. You can't buy an IRA and you can't sell an IRA. You can buy investments and have them held in an IRA, but an IRA is NEVER the investment. This is a common misconception among IRA holders, and it's one that can cost them (and you) tens or even hundreds of thousands of dollars.
4. The correct answer is B. Anyone with earned income. That's right, all it takes is someone (even yourself) paying you for

work you've performed. Bear in mind that interest, dividends, inheritance, gifts, rents, and royalties are NOT earned income, therefore cannot be contributed to a retirement plan. We will discuss the full ramifications of this later.

5. Let's start by determining what constitutes retirement. 70 ½ is the age you MUST start taking minimum distributions from your IRA, 403B, or 401K. 65 seems to stick in a lot of people's minds because that used to be the age for mandatory retirement. At 62, you can start receiving Social Security. And at age 59 ½ you may take penalty free distributions from your retirement accounts. None of these are good working definitions of retirement. For the purpose of this book, and hopefully for the rest of your life, retirement happens when you stop doing what you HAVE to do and start doing what you **LOVE** to do! If you're very blessed, those will always be the same thing. But for the purposes of retirement plans, there IS a way to take distributions before age 59 ½ without penalty. So the answer is TRUE!
6. FALSE!!! Any plan can do business with any other plan! You don't have much money in your IRA? Your IRA can partner with your wife's Roth, and they both can partner with your daughter's Coverdell ESA, and they all can partner with your father-in-law's 401K! And they can invest in just about anything you can imagine.
7. TRUE!! Commingling is strictly illegal. Remember in the foreword where I said this is a team sport? You need a

really GREAT (good isn't good enough) accountant. The bookkeeping is simple, but it has to be done correctly. Combine – Yes! Commingle – No!

8. Freebie! You get this one right no matter how you answered! Remember when you were in school, and every once in a while a teacher would pass out a test, but one of the questions had an error on it, so regardless of how you answered the question, you got it right? Well this is one of those times. There is no such thing as "Pull money out" or "Take money out" of a retirement plan. There are distributions. When you hear someone say "I'm gonna pull money out of my IRA" or "I had to take money out of my IRA" you know you are talking to someone who is making or has made a HUGE mistake.
9. D. Yep, just about anything. There are only 4 classes of investments that can't go in, and this question lists three of them.
10. FALSE! No matter how goofy your brother-in-law is, he can run a pizza parlor out of his IRA. He just can't work there. Or eat there. And if it's a Roth IRA, neither can you.
11. C. Newborn to Methuselah! Let's say you filmed your next kid's birth, then sold the film to the hospital for training purposes. As soon as you apply for the Social Security Number for your new little one, you can pay your newborn so then he or she could deposit it into a retirement plan. Oh, don't forget to give your child a name also. Unlike traditional IRAs (TIRA), which prohibit contributions after 70, there is no age based contribution restriction on a Roth.

Ok, this is how to grade yourself. If you saw some humor in this test, and enjoyed opening your mind to new possibilities, give yourself an A. If you got all hung up on what you got right or wrong, give yourself an F. And circle it.

An Artificial Distinction

For the purposes of this book, we will consider only two attributes of IRAs regardless of their type. Individual IRAs, SEP-IRAs, SIMPLE IRAs, SAR-SEP IRAs, Keoughs and 403(b)s all have one common trait: All contributions are given a tax deduction up front, when the contribution is made. All contributions and profit become taxable upon distribution. Think “No Tax Now – Tax Later.” This is the distinction that unifies this group. There are differences that separate each of these as well. Keoughs and SARSEP IRAs have been discontinued and can only be maintained by employers, but may not be established as new plans. 403(b)s, also known as TSAs or TDAs, can only be established by non-profit organizations and make contributions through salary reduction. SEP-IRAs and SIMPLE IRAs are established by small businesses to give their employees a retirement plan. Self direction is appropriate only for Individual IRAs and not for employer sponsored plans.

Since the United States has become a nation of job-hoppers, most people have plans with former employers. If a person changed jobs three times in the last 15 years, it’s conceivable that he could have a Keough, a SARSEP, a SEP and an individual IRA all with balances in them. To be able to self direct any of these accounts, all old plans through employers must be transferred to an individual IRA.

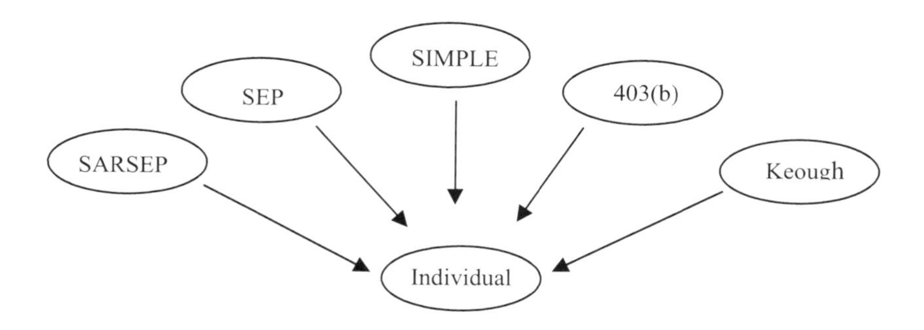

Most people don't realize that these transfers can be done and that they must be done to self direct the account. To roll from any of these accounts to an individual IRA, a person must experience one of the three Ds – Death, Disability or Discharge. The first two hopefully won't befall you any time soon. For most of us, discharge, that is, separation of service or loss of employment, will be the key to allowing a person to roll accounts to a self directed individual IRA.

Roth IRAs are given no tax deduction for the contribution, therefore contributions and profit escape taxation upon distribution. Think "Tax Now – No Tax Ever Again!"

Since self-direction is not appropriate for employer sponsored plans, this book will only address individual IRAs and Roth IRAs. So for our purposes, all non-Roths are simply IRAs.

As you make your way through this book, you will discover that there is a lot of misinformation circulating about retirement plans, much of it promulgated by "professionals". Brokers, insurance agents and bankers simply never have to deal with most of the aspects of a retirement plan because they deal with investments that never generate the need for knowledge of these issues. Worse yet, most of the investments available to you don't or can't pay these professionals, so they never gain knowledge about them as alternatives. The system of professionals inherently limits the information available to investors, constricting their knowledge, thereby limiting their freedom. Even CPAs have limited knowledge because so few of them deal with investors committed to self determination.

You may ask "Why doesn't everyone know this stuff?" That's a very legitimate question and the answer is this – The farmer who has a surplus of hay to sell to another region of the country affected by drought isn't advertising on prime time TV to let you know you can do that. The guy whose house is going into foreclosure isn't running ads on the Superbowl telling you what a good investment that would be. People with run down mobile homes don't promote in the paper or in Kiplinger's Magazine that you can buy their unit for a little bit of nothing, have it refurbished then sell it at a profit in your 401K (I know of one man who does just that). So again, knowledge is freedom. The people who control the knowledge control the market. By the way, those people are at a great party that you're paying for. The sad thing is, you're not invited to their party.

Points to Remember

1. You can't buy an IRA.
2. IRAs don't make or lose money. Investments make and lose money.
3. An IRA is a trust.
4. Only earned income can be contributed to an IRA.
5. Only non-employer plans can be self-directed.

4. Trust Me!

IRAs, Roth IRAs, SIMPLE IRAs, SEP-IRAs, 403Bs (sometimes called TSAs or TDAs), HSAs, 401Ks and Coverdell ESAs (formerly known as Educational IRAs) are all organized under trust law. So to be perfectly accurate, these plans are types of trusts given favorable tax treatment in the IRS code. There are many types of trusts, most of which are defined by the purpose of the trust. Furthermore, a trust is a legal entity. You are a legal entity (if you're older than 18 and are competent), corporations are legal entities, and trusts are legal entities. What differentiates trusts from other legal entities is this: Trusts only exist as long as they own something. No matter how much documentation is generated, no matter how many legal filings there are, if the trust doesn't own anything, it doesn't exist.

This is a common dodge used by nefarious attorneys involved in estate planning. The American Association of Retired People (AARP) recommends trusts for most retirees. This is great advice for the most part, and is given to help folks avoid probate and reduce some estate taxes. I have, however, sat down with retirees and been told they have set up trusts. When asked if they've titled their house to the trust, they say "No." Have they changed their savings and checking accounts to the trust? Again "No." Stocks, bonds, mutual funds, other property, vacation home, RV? "No, no, and no."

In the case above, the retired couple paid for a trust, but were never told they needed to "fund" the trust, that is, they needed to retitle accounts and property to the trust. If they had passed away, their estate would have gone through probate and the attorney would not only have charged them for a trust, they would have had to pay attorney's fees for the probate proceedings.

In another case, the people went to a lawyer and had documents drawn up. Upon reviewing them I found that the attorney had drafted wills that created trusts upon their deaths. These people didn't have the documents set up that would allow them to establish the trust, even if they had wanted to fund it. One of them had to die first.

So keep in mind that an IRA and most of the related retirement accounts are trusts, and as such they have to own something to exist. As long as they own something, trusts can exist into perpetuity.

In case this still isn't clear, let's imagine that you have a garage. Your motorcycle is parked in your garage, and one morning you put your cycle key into the garage door. Not only does the garage sit there doing nothing, you can't even open the garage door with a motorcycle key. You would never mistake your garage for your cycle or vice versa. In this example, your cycle is your investment and your garage is your tax advantaged trust. Just as your garage protects your motorcycle from dust, wind, rain, hail and UV rays, your IRA protects your investments from the effect of taxes. So to run the garage analogy to its extreme, let's imagine that you have a car that you only drive in parades. It's so valuable that you keep it in a secured garage. It's under a tarp and the garage owner has installed a fantastic security system. It's so restricted that even you have to undergo many checks and double checks to get access to your vehicle. I've just described an IRA, and the garage owner is your custodian. Your custodian manages the garage, you manage your vehicle. (Folks, this is an analogy. In reality, you can't invest in collectible cars in your IRA.)

The custodian of an IRA performs ministerial duties (IRS speak), that is, the custodian makes sure all the correct documents are filed with the IRS, investments are properly titled, and whatever needs reporting gets reported. BUT …and this is a BIG BUT ….. they can also limit what a person may invest in. They may not tell you WHAT to invest in, but they can certainly tell you what you may NOT invest in.

So to make things perfectly clear, or as clear as this subject will allow, let's look at the IRS rules first.

Restricted Investments

The following is the list of investments you may not put in your IRA. It is far easier to list what you may not put in, than what you may put in, because there are really only four classes of restricted investments.

1. Collectibles – antiques, cars (don't be confused by the example, it was just an analogy), jewelry, art, rugs, stamps, grandma's thimble collection, plates, alcohol (*really, the IRS code lists alcohol. I thought alcohol was consumable, not collectible, but what do I know?*), coins (*ok, there are classes of coins minted specifically for IRAs made of gold, silver, as well as platinum and palladium bars, but they must be held at a secured repository. However that wheat penny you found in your change can't go in*), bobble head dolls, etc.

2. S-Corps. IRAs don't exclude S-Corps (Corporations electing to be taxed under Subchapter S of the IRS code), but the rules of S-Corps exclude IRAs. Either way, an IRA may not hold

stock in an S-Corp. IRAs may hold membership in Limited Liability Companies (LLC), and they should if the IRA is going to invest in real estate.

3. Insurance. No life, health, long term care, disability, etc. An IRA may purchase property and casualty insurance on investments requiring it, such as real estate.

4. No investment incurring unlimited liability. Okay, in regular terms, it means no uncovered calls (a type of stock option trade), speculation in futures contracts or some types of derivatives. You may use futures to hedge if your IRA owns the underlying investment, but you may not speculate with these contracts. You may not sell short, and for IRAs, no buying on margin.

Okay, so that's it. That's what you can't invest in. Want to buy and sell cattle? Import clocks from China? Own a 62 unit apartment building? Run a pizza parlor? Sell T-Shirts on the internet? If you can dream it, you can do it. (*Running a business incurs a little known tax, so you might not want to do that anyway, but the point is, you can if you choose to.*)
But not if your custodian says you can't. When you hear the term IRA, what do you think of immediately? If you're like most people, you think of brokerage firms, banks, or insurance companies. The custodians for these companies will make sure that you continue to think of them, because if you go to your current IRA custodian and tell them you want to trade exotic chickens in your IRA, they'll tell you that you can't do that.

But the truth of the matter is, THEY can't do that: you can. You just need a better custodian.

So this is your assignment. Go to the internet. Type "Self Directed Custodian" into Google. You'll see that there are a few custodians out there that allow you to manage your own investments through them. The only thing better than having the right custodian, is becoming your own trustee. You can't do that in an IRA, but there is a better option available now. We'll discover that shortly.

We're also going to discover a hidden and obscure tax that looms inside IRAs. We'll get to know Unrelated Business Income Tax soon.

So now you should know the difference between your retirement plan and the underlying investment. If you hear someone say "I have to pull money out" of my IRA, give them this book. They really need to know the difference.

Points to Remember

1. All retirement plans are trusts.
2. Only four restricted investments in an IRA.
    - Collectibles
    - Insurance
    - S-Corps
    - Unlimited Liability Investments
3. Any transaction you can make outside your retirement plan, you can make inside your retirement plan.

4. You are not limited to stocks, bonds, mutual funds, or any other Wall Street fabrications.
5. You can invest in your area of expertise.
6. You can lend to, co-own, become equity partners in any business endeavor.

5. "Pulling Money Out"

By mistaking their investment for their IRA, people make huge and costly mistakes. Two women came to my seminar about a month apart. The first woman, we'll call Kate, had just taken a distribution (the correct way of referring to this transaction) or "pulled money out" (the incorrect way of referring to this transaction) of her IRA. She "pulled her money out" because her investment was doing so poorly (in her mind her "IRA" was doing poorly). So to put it in her parlance, she "pulled her money out" because her "IRA" wasn't doing well.

What really happened was this. She took a distribution from her IRA because her investment was doing poorly. She didn't understand that she could have transferred the investment to something more secure, leaving it inside the protection of the IRA.

"Well, couldn't she put it back in?" I hear you ask, and the answer is "YES!"

"MAYBE!"

IRA custodians may withhold 10% of the distributions unless the participant fills out paperwork to do otherwise. So in Kate's example she "pulled $10,000 out" of her IRA and the custodian withheld 10% to send to Uncle Sam. Kate didn't realize that

- She had 60 days to "put the money back in" to an IRA.
- She had to "put in" the entire $10,000.

The $1,000 that the custodian had withheld, even though it was sent to the IRS, still counted as a distribution. So Kate's scenario could have looked like this:

Amount of Distribution	$10,000
10% Withholding	-$1,000 (sent to the IRS)
New IRA Rollover	$9,000

If Kate had "taken out" $10,000, and rolled over $9,000. This would have resulted in a taxable distribution of $1,000 EVEN THOUGH THE MONEY WAS AT THE IRS! If Kate were in a 25% tax bracket, she would owe $250 in taxes on that $1,000, and since she was younger than 59 ½, she would owe $100.00 for the 10% penalty. This misunderstanding could have cost her $350.

"Couldn't her broker have helped her?" I hear you ask, and the answer is "YES, he should have, but didn't." A simple question like "Why do you want to take a distribution?" would have cleared all of that up. If asked that question, Kate could have told him that she was dissatisfied with the performance of her current investment, and he could have guided her to something safer ALL INSIDE HER IRA!

But the question was never asked. Kate took a distribution and the firm withheld 10% because nobody took the second opportunity to ask her that question while offering her the option of filling out the paperwork to escape the withholding. Because Kate attended one of my seminars just days after this incident, she alerted the firm, thus they were able to stop the transfer of the withholding to the IRS. Kate was able to take the entire distribution to roll over to her new investment inside a new IRA. Kate had 60 days to do this, so avoided another pitfall by handling it quickly.

Allie wasn't so lucky. Allie attended my seminar about a month after Kate. She had taken a distribution from her IRA because she was dissatisfied with the investment's performance (do you see the pattern - People confusing the investment's performance with the IRA's performance?). She took a distribution of $15,000, and the custodian withheld $1,500 (again, two missed opportunities to correctly counsel the client). Unfortunately for Allie, the firm had already wired the withholding to the IRS. Now of course, she could get her withholding back, but only upon filing her tax return for that year. Because this happened in June, she would be well beyond the 60 day limit by the time she filed her taxes in January.

So because of ignorance on Allie's part and neglect on the part of her broker and custodian, Allie received $13,500 of her $15,000 distribution. She rolled over $13,500 to her new IRA and paid 25% of the $1,500 in taxes and $150.00 for the ten percent penalty, totaling $525.00 for this mistake.

Please note that any time I use the term "pull money out" or "take money out" I use quotation marks. There is no such thing as "pull money out" or "take money out" of a retirement plan. There are distributions. Most distributions are painful and costly. Ask Kate and Allie. Fortunately for both of them, they were working with relatively small dollars. What if they had $100,000 IRAs? Do you see the implications?

From now on I will not use the terms "pull money out" or "take money out", the correct term is distribution. As a matter of fact, we'll stop using the term "out" entirely. This book is designed to educate you on how to use the money IN your retirement plan to its best advantage. So we will kick "out" out of your vocabulary. But first we'll consider distributions.

1. Lump Sum Distribution –

Sometimes called the "lunk head" distribution. There may be times that it's absolutely necessary for people to take a large withdrawal from their retirement plan, but there are provisions that allow for many of them, and for the most part, these types of distributions come from financial stress, poor planning and ignorance.

Take the case of Ed and Shirley. Their last child has left the home, and now they want to upgrade their furniture. They've had their eye on a suite for their living room, all leather, and it's only $6,000.00. Ed doesn't want to put it on his credit card and pay 18% for it, but he's got that one IRA that isn't doing very well anyway, and besides, he can't get at the money 'til he's 59 ½, so.... He "pulls the money out" of his IRA to pay for the suite. $6,000 taken as a lump sum distribution incurs $1,500 taxes in the 25% tax bracket. Add in $600 for the 10% penalty and Ed has incurred $2,100 in costs to get his $6,000 furniture. That's a nice, tidy 35%. Quite a savings over his 18% credit card, right?

You can see that lump sum distributions are costly. Ed not only spent an extra $2,100 for his furniture, but while that suite is depreciating toward $0, his $6,000 is gone and can't earn anything else in the future. This is a classic lose-lose-lose situation.

2. Education Distribution –

You, your spouse, or your kids can use a distribution for education. You must make sure that the eligible student attends an IRS approved institution. This is any college, university, vocational school or other POST-secondary school that meets federal student aid requirements. It can be public, private or non-profit as long as it's accredited. You pay tax, but no penalty.

3. **First Time Home Buyer Distribution**–

You must not have owned a home for the previous two years. You may take up to a $10,000 distribution from your own IRA, or your spouse's, parent's, or children's IRAs. If your spouse qualifies, you can double that. If you withdraw from a Roth, the Roth must have been established for at least five years. Applicable taxes are incurred, but no penalty.

4. **Distributions for Total and Permanent Disability** –

If you become totally disabled, you may take withdrawals from your IRA penalty free. Applicable taxes remain intact. If you're withdrawing from a Roth, the 5 year rule still applies.

Did you know that under SSDI rules, a person can have unlimited assets AND unlimited income as long as the income is UNEARNED (think rental income!).

5. **Distributions for Reimbursement of Unpaid Medical Expenses** –

Taxes applied, but penalty free. Roth 5 year rule applies.

6. **Payment of Health Insurance Premiums While Unemployed** –

Taxes incurred, penalty free. Roth 5 year rule applies.

7. **Death** –

Taxes incurred by traditional IRA. No penalties for Roths or Traditional accounts.

So those are the distributions one can take from Roths and TIRAs. Since nothing is as simple as it seems, the rules regarding Roth distributions can be quite involved. A handy guide for early Roth distributions has been included in the back of the book.

60 Day Rollovers

When is a distribution not a distribution? When it's a 60 day rollover.

You may take a distribution from you IRA or your Roth, use it for something, then redeposit it into the same or similar type of account. But beware! You have 60 days!

How many months is 60 days?

If you answered "two", then you are in big trouble. The only time two months adds to 60 days is once every 4 years when February has 29 days. The rest of the time two months can add to 58, 61 and 62 days. The IRS will give you until April 16th to file your income tax if the 15th falls on a Sunday, but they will never give you an extra day for a 60 day rollover. (There actually is an exception, but it occurs so rarely as to be non-existent.)

Worse yet, 60 days may not be 60 days at all. Let's say Larry receives his distribution on May 7th, 2009. He plans to use the money for a brief time, and deposit it back into his IRA in 60 days. He looks at the calendar and finds the 60th day is Monday, July 6th. He plans to the minute when he will get his deposit back into the IRA he has established at his local bank. He uses his local bank so he doesn't have to worry about checks lost in the mail or wiring expenses. On Monday July 6th, 2009, Larry drives to his bank, then tries to calm the sinking feeling in the pit of his stomach. Because the 4th of July fell on a Saturday that year, the banks and all financial institutions take their holiday the following Monday! Oops. Tuesday is the 61st day, and Larry has no grace period. In this case Larry's 60 day rollover really was a 57 day rollover, but now it's not a rollover at all. It's become a lump sum distribution with taxes and penalties.

In reality, the 60 day rollover IS a lump sum distribution, until you prove otherwise. There are some uses for it, but for the most part it is fraught with danger. You can see that for most people, the lump sum distribution is the one most easily abused and misunderstood. Now if you hear that horrible phrase "I'm gonna have to pull money out …." you can do something for that person. Don't just give them this book, let them know what you're doing with your investments and retirement program. Remember, at this party, you have to bring friends.

Points to Remember

1. There is no such thing as "pulling money out" or "taking money out."
2. Withdrawals from retirement plans are properly called distributions.
3. Lump sum distributions are usually detrimental.
4. There are some distributions taken before 59 ½ that escape penalties.
5. A 60 day roll over is a distribution that is taken, then re-deposited in 60 days.
6. If a 60 day rollover is deposited in 60 days, it escapes penalty.

7. If a 60 day rollover is deposited after 60 days, it becomes a lump sum distribution, it becomes taxable, and it incurs a 10% penalty if before 59 ½.
8. 60 day rollovers have specific uses, but can be dangerous and should be avoided.

6. The Last of the Don'ts

Even the wildest party has rules. Don't run in the neighbor's yard. Don't use our good guest towels. Don't go through my wife's dresser. Don't jump out of the convertible while it's moving. We've covered a few don'ts, you remember: the four things we can't invest in; why not to take lump sum distributions; why to avoid 60 day rollovers. This chapter will be the last cautionary word, and after that, we'll investigate the true power of these plans.

Restricted Transactions –

Whereas there were only four classes as far as restricted investments go, there are limitless transactions that are restricted. The reason they're limitless is because they're situational, that is, they arise with every opportunity and can result in confusion. But there are three simple rules that apply.

1. You may not do business directly with your own retirement plan.
2. You may not get a secondary benefit from your retirement plan.
3. You may not make non-cash contributions to your plan.
4. All other rules are based on these three rules.

Yes, in the great scope of things, YOU are restricted. You may not buy from, sell to, borrow money from, lend money to, gain benefit in any manner from, or make non-cash contributions to your IRA, Roth, SIMPLE, SEP, CESA, HSA or 401K. Neither can your family. Let's take a look at the people who are restricted.

1. Fiduciary, counsel or employee of the plan – Ok, so if ABC Bank is the custodian of your IRA, you may not buy ABC Bank Stock.
2. Persons providing services to your plan – Bill is the President of ABC Bank. He has a house for sale. Your plan cannot buy his house. It can buy many other houses, but not his.
3. An employer of whom any employees are covered by the plan. Jill has a self directed IRA. She wants to make a promissory note as an investment. She can lend money to many people in this regard, but she can't lend money to her boss. This is an actual case where a client of mine wanted to lend money to her employer. Even though the project he wanted the money for was unrelated to the business where she worked, he is restricted.
4. Employee organizations whose members are covered by the plan.
5. Business entities or trusts that are 50% owned by restricted individuals.
6. Officers, directors, 10% or more shareholders and employees of any restricted individuals or organizations.
7. A partner or joint-venturer who owns 10% along with any restricted party.
8. Lineal antecedents or descendents, spouses, and in the case of Roth IRAs, brothers and sisters. In short: family.

Let's look at some real life examples.

Hannah and her Brother –

Hannah has a small IRA. Her brother wanted to borrow $10,000 from her. She checked the rules and found that since her IRA was traditional, she could legally lend to her sibling. If it had been a Roth, he would have been restricted. She wrote a promissory note, sent the note along with a letter of intent to the custodian, and lent her brother $10,000. Everything's fine, right?

The terms were that the note was to be paid back, plus interest, at the end of a year. Her brother didn't pay her back. Her only recourse now was to file against him in court and start collection proceedings. She has no choice. If she were to let it slide (it's her brother, after all), then the IRS would step in and looking at the facts of the case, determine that she had violated their code.

Why? She certainly didn't benefit from it financially. She's out $10,000, the interest her brother owes her, and she's out what she could have earned elsewhere. But none of that has any bearing on the violation. First, the fact that the distribution went to her brother is highly suspect (not illegal, just suspect). What's to say he didn't give her the money back for her own use? Why is she not filing against him? If this loan had been made more than arm's length, it would seem less suspicious. But of course, if it had been made to an unrelated individual, she would have filed and begun collection proceedings. So even though we can't prove that the money went somewhere besides back to her, she is developing a secondary benefit – Family Harmony!

Let's look at another example.

Jenny and her Sister –

Jenny has bought a rental property in her Traditional IRA. Her sister Jill, whom she loves, wants to move into the house and rent it. It's not a Roth, so she lets Jill move in dragging along Howie. Howie is Jill's husband and Jenny's brother-in-law, and although Jenny loves Jill, Jenny finds Jill's taste in men questionable. Jill and Howie pay rent for three months, and everything seems fine, but the fourth month there's no rent. The fifth month there's no rent also, but Jill calls Jenny one night and cries "Please let us stay here. Howie's laid off right now, but he's got a bunch of résumés out and he's working part time at the fast food place, so we should be able to make things right soon."

What must Jenny do? She must start eviction proceedings against them. If she doesn't, she's generated a secondary benefit from her IRA. Even though she's out three months rent, and has suffered a financial loss, the IRS would consider the fact that her sister is staying there rent free as a secondary benefit to Jenny. It's that darned Family Harmony again.

So you can see that even though something is allowed by law, it may not be worth the trouble. A quick note on Jenny's house: Jenny can manage the house, she can collect the rents on behalf of her IRA, but she may not do any work on the house. She can't paint, patch holes, sweep the floor or mow the lawn. And if Jenny should happen to own a property management company, that company can't do any of that work either.

Any property you own in your plan is completely off limits to you. You can't stay in your vacation home near Orlando, but you can rent it to anyone on the planet except your immediate family.

Let's go over those people one more time, your grandparents, your parents, your spouse, your spouse's parents, your spouse's grandparents, your kids, your grandkids, your great-grand children and in the case of a Roth, your and your spouse's brothers and sisters. (I gave a presentation last night where someone asked "What about step sisters?" So, for you picky individuals, step-brothers, step-sisters, half-brothers, half-sisters, ex-wives, ex-husbands, parent's ex-wives, parents' ex-husbands, kids' ex – oh, I think you've got it by now.)

Hey, what about my cousins or my nieces and nephews? Hey, what about your uncles and aunts? Hey! None of them are restricted. So if your uncle is a plumber, and that house you just bought in your kid's Coverdell ESA needs plumbing, knock yourself out! You can hire him for all your plumbing needs.

Your Hero

Your new hero for all these transactions is a fellow by the name of Al Capone.

Here's why. Although he was never successfully convicted of racketeering, boot legging, murder, extortion, or arson, Al Capone's career ended in 1931 when he was indicted and convicted by the Federal Government of Income Tax Evasion!

Yes, the FBI chased him, but it was the IRS that caught him.

The rules and their applications regarding retirement accounts are so powerful that people really don't need to bend them to be profitable, or actually move beyond profitable. Playing by the rules is more than fun, and playing by the rules will keep you out of very hot water. Playing by the rules allows you to build true wealth currently and have access to it sooner than you think.

So there are many good reasons to follow the rules. Here are three very bad reasons to follow them. The IRS takes a very dim view on people who ignore or violate their rules. Their punishment is extreme and costly. Avoiding these sanctions will keep you very happy.

In the event of violating these rules, the IRS can:

1. Disallow the investment.
2. Impose a $100,000.00 fine
3. Dissolve the IRA

Furthermore, if someone has performed a restricted transaction, that is, their retirement plan has done business with a disallowed individual, the IRS can impose a 15% prohibited transaction penalty on the amount of the investment, with a 100% penalty on those they deem recalcitrant.

Let's take a look at my friend Dan. Dan has an IRA of $320,000. Dan also owns a $90,000 cabin in Colorado he would dearly love to put in his IRA. Knowing that he can't do business directly with his IRA, he sells his cabin to his friend for $49,000 in 2006, his IRA buys his cabin from his friend for $50,000 in 2007. In 2010 he receives notice from the IRS that they've deemed the CIRCUMSTANCES of the sale to be in violation (Note: buying a cabin from a friend is not restricted, but arranging to circumnavigate the law is).

Since this arrangement is obviously intentional, the IRS would impose a 15% penalty on the $90,000 (they don't care that you bought it for $50,000, they use fair market value). Since each year is considered a separate violation, Dan incurs a $13,500 per year penalty for three years. Ouch! That's $40,500. Since Dan arranged the deal to circumnavigate the law, the IRS could impose a 100% penalty as well. Pretty good going, Dan. You've just incurred $130,500 in penalties and taxes for trying to fool the IRS.

Oh, but it gets worse. When they make Dan distribute the cabin from his IRA, thereby disallowing it, he gets to add $90,000 to his current income. If he's in a 25% tax bracket, this could push him into a 28% bracket. 28% of $90,000 is $25,200, AND he has a 10% early withdrawal penalty, since Dan is not 59 ½ years old. That's another $34,200 on top of his $130,500.

Did we mention the $100,000 penalty? We're now up to $264,700.

But the IRS doesn't mess around. In all likelihood they would dissolve Dan's IRA. Let's see, we have $320,000 added to his current income. That puts Dan in the 35% tax bracket. If Dan earned $100,000 in 2010, he would owe the IRS $124,644 just in regular income tax, plus his $100,000 fine, plus $130,500 for his restricted transaction penalty. If my math is correct, Dan owes $355,144.

Do you see that playing by the rules is fun and profitable? Ignoring the rules is painful. So my commitment to you is that everything you read in this book will pass the Al Capone test.

If you're going to party, we want you to party safely.

Ok, that's my friend, Dan. What if a couple buys a resort property outside of Orlando? Why couldn't the family enjoy it for two weeks out of the year? Really, think about it, are there really IRS agents crawling around outside of Disneyworld checking out this sort of thing?

That was a question asked at a seminar given by a firm that provides custodial services to retirement plans. Here is the representatives answer:

"I'm not going to tell you that you can or you can't. It depends on your risk tolerance. Are there IRS agents everywhere? Obviously not. So it's really up to you if you want to do it."

When asked the same question, this is my answer:

"I know your marriage is rock solid, and will never fail. But in every family there's that one brother who's a great guy, but his taste in life partners is questionable. Furthermore, his wife hates your wife for no known reason. When your sister-in-law finally files for divorce and she finds out she gets 10% of everything the IRS collects from her tip, you can bet she's going to turn you in. Let's see, a $500,00 IRA taxed at 35% is $165,000 dollars, plus the $100,000 fine, um, that adds up to $265,000. Now, if she gets 10%, that $26,500 buys a mighty fine divorce. Your kids very nicely sent pictures of themselves to their cousins in front of the house or back in the pool, and those pictures are now on Facebook and your kids personal webpages, as well as stored in your computer.

Oh, you don't have any siblings? What about the property manager that gets ticked off at you, or one of your tenants over some silly dispute? Are there IRS agents everywhere? Not now, but man, they pop up like crazy.

My point is that it has nothing to do with risk tolerance. Would you tell someone who's thinking of selling drugs out of the trunk of his car to the elementary school kids "Well, it depends on your risk tolerance?"
Follow the rules: party safely, party well.

Quick Knowledge Check

1. IRAs (any kind), HSAs, 401Ks and Coverdell ESAs are not investments. They are accounts that can be established, then allowed to be tax advantaged.
2. IRAs (any kind), HSAs, and Coverdell ESAs are types of trusts. All these are established under trust law, and must function as trusts.
3. Trusts need custodians. Custodians do all the behind the scenes legal stuff.
4. Custodians do NOT manage investments; they manage trusts.
5. Your custodian will not tell you what to invest in, but they may dictate what you may NOT invest in.
6. You must pick the right custodian.
7. You can invest in anything you can imagine, except collectibles, insurance, S-Corps, or certain transactions that incur unlimited liability.
8. Most distributions are costly and negative, especially lump sum distributions.
9. Violations are costly and negative, but can be easily avoided simply by following the rules.
10. You now know more than most people who have IRAs and probably know more than most people who call themselves professionals.

I know number 10 is a bold statement, but there is so much misinformation about these accounts, that it takes very little to exceed others' incorrect knowledge.

Points to Remember

1. Unlike restricted investments, restricted transactions are numerous.
2. The possibility of restricted transactions arise with every investment opportunity.
3. The penalties are punitive.
4. The IRS is unforgiving.
5. The power of using retirement plans is so great, there is no need to "bend" the rules.
6. There is no "bending" the rules. The IRS doesn't bend.
7. All IRAs need custodians.
8. Custodians charge fees to IRAs.

7. The Good Stuff

Life just gets better from this chapter on. There is so much you can do with your retirement money that you don't even know or suspect. You can start earning returns much better than those available in the market, and if you do things right, your plan can garner you current income! You will find that your plan can partner with many others to increase your investment potential.

So we've covered all the restricted people, that is, people your plan can't do business with, right? Well here's a new rule. ANY plan can do business with ANY OTHER PLAN!. Let me stress this again. ANY plan can do business with ANY OTHER PLAN! Plans are never restricted, ever. Your father's traditional IRA can do business with your son's Coverdell ESA, your Roth IRA can do business with your mother's Health Savings Account, your Solo 401K can co-invest with all of the above. Furthermore, all those plans can all get together and co-invest in projects, so that everyone can benefit.

This is so important, I'm going to say it again – ANY PLAN can do business with ANY OTHER PLAN!

Let's get to basics – we need to understand some things so that we don't get confused later on when we look at how wonderful these plans are.

Earned Income: That's easy, it's income that's earned! Think "work". W-2 income is earned income. Some 1099 income is earned, such as commissions or work performed as an independent contractor, not as an employee. Tips are earned income. Income stated on your Schedule C is earned income. What is NOT earned income? Inheritance, royalties, rents, gambling proceeds, insurance proceeds, interest, dividends, long term capital gains, to name a few.

Why do we need to know the difference? Because all retirement plans are based on Earned Income. Except for the Coverdell ESA, all plans require contributions made from earned income. If I earn $100,000 this year (note the word earn), I can contribute (note the word contribute), a portion of that to an IRA, a Roth, a 401K, or an HSA. If I inherit $100,000 this year, I can contribute nothing! That's right, Nada, Zip, Zilch. $100,000 in interest? Nada, Zip, Zilch. My stock went up by $100,000? NZZ.

Contributions: Contributions are the portion of my earned income that I can deposit into my account. So if I'm 45 and I earn $75,000 this year, I can CONTRIBUTE $5,000 to my traditional IRA, or $5,000 to my Roth IRA, or $15,500 to my 401K. Think of money OUTSIDE the plan being put INTO the plan. There are limits on contributions.

Remember as you read this: There are limits on CONTRIBUTIONS. There are NO limits on profits. Write this down somewhere. Put it on your bathroom mirror in so you can see it before you go to bed at night and when you get up in the morning. There are limits on contributions, not on PROFIT!

Your IRA can earn as much as it wants, or as much as you want. If you buy a house in your IRA for $175,000, put $25,000 into fixing it up, then sell it for $250,000 your IRA just earned $50,000. Since all of that transaction took place within your plan, (the house was bought in your plan, the work was done in your plan and paid for by your plan, the house was sold in your plan and the title company cut the check to your plan) then NONE of that is a contribution. It's all PROFIT that occurs within the plan.

Some people have a huge difficulty wrapping their minds around this. Imagine that you CONTRIBUTED $500 to your IRA and invest it immediately in MJM Industrials, Ltd. You buy 100 shares at a nickel a piece (yeah, I know, there're commissions, but you'll get the idea), and immediately MJM with their cure for the common cold, skyrockets to $1,000 per share. Your IRA is now worth $100,000. That's great! Good for you and all those cold sufferers. Now here's the question – What was your contribution?

If you said $500, then you were right. You only put $500 of your earned income into the plan, regardless of how your plan profited. You earned tens of thousands of dollars profits, but made only $500 in contributions. This example is truly a faerie tale, no one ever makes those profits on one stock, but it demonstrates the difference between contributions and profit. So again, there are limits on contributions, but there are no limits on profits within the plan.

I can't stress this enough. I have had so many people in the middle of a presentation, ask "Aren't you limited to $5,000 per year (for an IRA)?" when shown the profit on a single real estate transaction. They have obviously confused ______________ for ______________.

As we make our way through the examples, it's good to be clear on this because we're going to delve into the math of all this. I know, most people hate math, but the better we are at math, the better our returns and ultimately, the better our life will be.

Here's one more quick note. Take "out" out of your vocabulary. We will not be taking money "out" of our plans (with one exception). All the transactions we'll investigate occur IN the plans. Our IRAs, HSAs, Roths, and 401Ks will invest in properties, and these plans will keep all the profits. Remember from an earlier chapter, when we heard people say "I'm gonna pull money OUT of my IRA," it meant trouble? We will never take money OUT.

So now we should know:

1. What earned income is.
2. What a contribution is.
3. What profit is.
4. Where all our transactions take place.

So in short, we earn some income through work. We take a piece of that earned income and make a contribution to our plan. Once the plan is funded with our contribution, we direct those funds into real estate (or some other profitable endeavor), which is bought or sold or rented INSIDE the plan, creating profit that STAYS in the plan, making our plan bigger and better and more capable of taking care of us. Understanding this allows us to plan for the party.

8. Math for Fun and Profit

"Life is story problems."

I ask you, dear reader, to bear with me here. I know most people's eyes glaze over and the attention span shortens to milliseconds when math is mentioned, but I will endeavor to make our math as painless as possible. Better yet, I would hope that by walking through this with me, you'll find that the math is really pretty simple, and greater still, enjoyable. I mean, you like to make money and have fun doing it, right?

So here's the situation. We'll talk about Annie. Annie Investor is a sharp young woman with a lot on the ball. She knows that mutual funds are not her friend and that the best place for her money is in an area where she has some experience or knowledge, thus the best manager for her money is Annie.

Annie opens her Roth IRA with $2,900. That's not the contribution limit, but it's all she's got. It is the contribution limit for a Health Savings Account (HSA) so this example works for HSAs too.

$2,900 isn't very much so she needs to find money somewhere else. Annie goes to her father. Annie's father has $140,000 in his traditional IRA (TIRA). Annie's father isn't satisfied with his returns because two years ago, his $140,000 was $230,000. She proposes this: "Dad, if your Traditional IRA (TIRA) will lend my Roth money, my Roth will pay your TIRA 10% on any money it lends." Dad is very pleased with this because that's 30% more than he made last year, and it's 2% more than his advisor tells him to expect long term from mutual funds.

Now remember, Annie is off limits from Dad's IRA, and Dad is off limits from Annie's Roth, but ANY PLAN can do business with ANY OTHER PLAN. Plans are NEVER off limits to each other. Since Dad's TIRA is doing business with Annie's Roth, this is a perfectly legal, legitimate transaction.

Annie's Roth	Dad's IRA
$2,900	$140,000

Annie finds a distressed property, a $200,000 house in need of TLC. She bargains the price down 40% getting an accepted offer of $120,000 for her Roth. Good job, Annie!

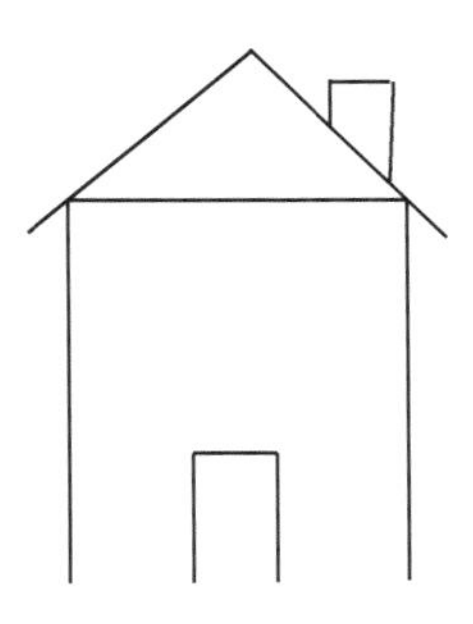

Annie's Roth borrows $117,100 from her Dad's traditional IRA and strikes a promissory note with it.

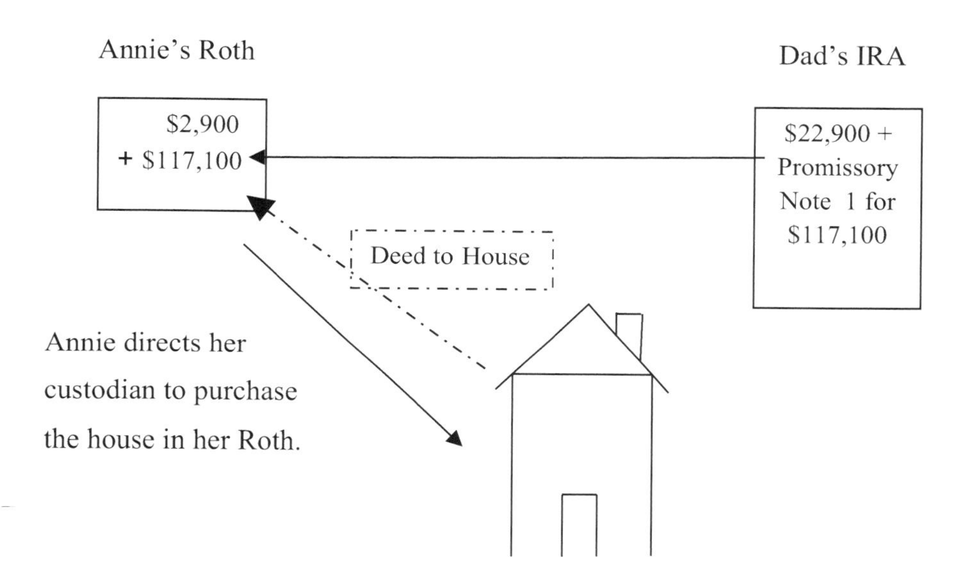

Notice that no money comes OUT of the Roth. The transaction takes place IN the Roth, just as if she had directed the custodian to buy mutual funds IN the Roth.

Even though Annie did a great job acquiring the house at a discount, she makes some mistakes as a new investor. To understand what she did, we need to clarify a couple of concepts.

Although Annie isn't interested in holding this house for very long, that is, she wants to "Flip" it, she doesn't understand the difference between a "Fix-n-Flip" and a "Rehab." A Fix-n-Flip consists of doing the minimal work needed to bring the house to code, then performing enough cosmetics to make the house desirable. In the parlance of Fix-n-Flippers, it's a matter of "Buying the pig, putting lipstick on the pig, then selling the pig." A typical Fix-n-Flip should cost a person $4,000 to $7,000, depending on how much labor is done and the cost of materials, and it should take about 6 – 8 weeks to accomplish.

A "Rehab" is much more intensive. Typically people rehab houses because they're either going to live there, or they're going to rent them to others for a long period. Since a landlord doesn't want ongoing repairs and increased maintenance costs, an investor will put more money into a distressed property for renting than a fix-n-flipper. This entails things such as installing new cabinets, new counter tops, improving bathroom fixtures, changing hollow core to solid wood doors, etc.

As a new investor Annie falls into the trap of loving the house more than she loves the numbers underlying her investment. Two things contribute to Annie's increased costs. First, Annie can do none of the work herself. Because this house is owned by her Roth, she cannot make a non-cash contribution to it, that is, she can do NONE of the work on the property. She can't paint, clean, or even mow the grass, so she must contract out for all of the work. But her big mistake comes from putting too much into the fix-n-flip for improving the property. No one told her that putting granite counter tops in a Formica neighborhood won't pay for itself.

Annie puts another $15,000 into the property. Because she doesn't have it in her own Roth, she borrows another $15,000 from her dad's IRA.

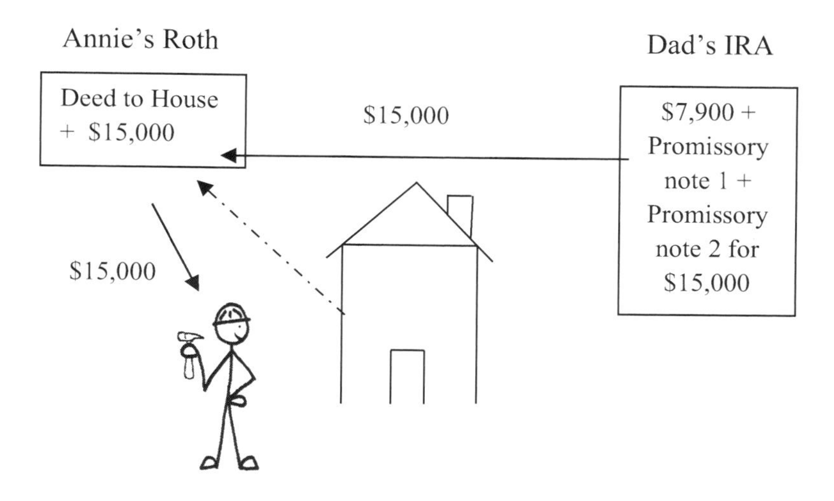

Another mistake that Annie makes is hiring the wrong contractor. A fix-n-flip should take 6 – 8 weeks, but our friendly handyman takes four months. FOUR MONTHS! This increases Annie's carrying costs, raises her expenses and decreases the overall profit she can make on this house. By listening to her contractor, Annie puts more into the project thereby drifting from fix-n-flip into rehab territory. Now we know why she's putting granite in a Formica neighborhood.

Expecting to get $200,000 for her house, after all that fixing, Annie's disappointed to net only $180,000 for the sale of the property. After paying realtor's fees, transfer fees, etc., Annie takes that $180,000 to pay off everyone.

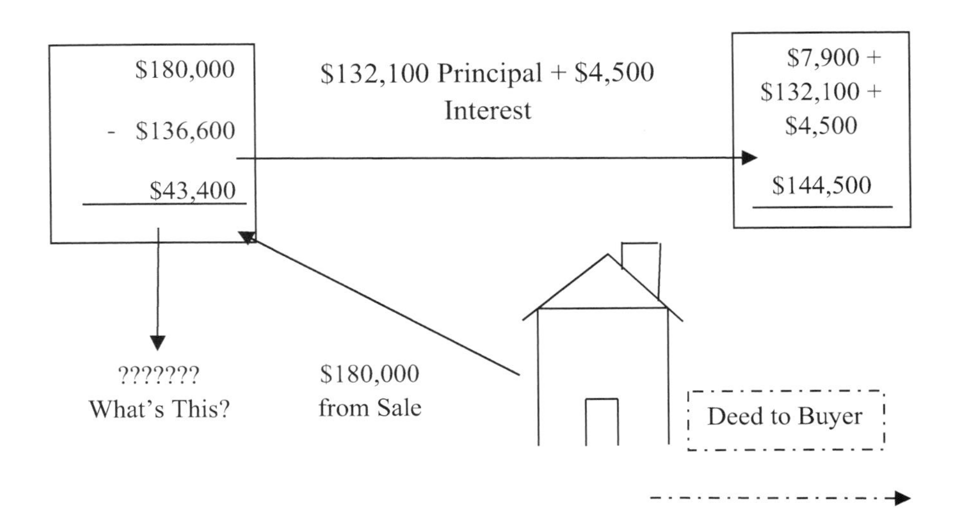

Let's take a look to see how Annie did.

Annie's Roth borrowed $132,100 in two notes from her father's IRA. She promised him 10%, which would be $13,210, and she accrued that interest over a third of a year leaving her owing $4,403.33. She loves her dad, and she doesn't like dealing with pennies, so she pays her dad a bonus of $97.67 bringing the total paid to her father of $4,500.00

$180,000 - Sale net of fees

Less	$2,900	Roth IRA Equity
	$132,100	Loan from Dad (includes purchase of house and improvements)
	$4,500	Interest Paid on Loan
	$139,500	Total Cost of Project

$40,500 Profit net Expenses

Annie's thrilled with her earnings, but there is an obscure tax waiting for her. ("What's This?" in the diagram)

All IRAs are organized under trust law (remember from Chapter 3?), and as such, transactions may be subject to Unrelated Business Income Tax (UBIT). Notice I said "May." Brokers are unfamiliar with UBIT because there's practically nothing they can invest your money in that will incur it. Real estate transactions may or may not incur it depending on the manner in which they're financed. If Annie had paid for the house and the rehab completely out of her own IRA without borrowing any money, she would have paid no UBIT. So how would she know if she is going to incur UBIT?

Let's follow the IRS' logic. They ask if Annie used Debt Financing for her project. Yes, Annie's Roth borrowed money from Dad's IRA, so she certainly used debt financing. Next they ask "Did she make any income?" Annie certainly made income; she made a profit of $40,500. So in the IRS' rules, Annie had Debt Financed Income, and since this is a trust, that type of income is called Unrelated Debt Financed Income (UDFI). UDFI is actually a calculation used to determine how much of her income or profit is taxable. Let's look at Annie's situation.

Annie's Roth borrowed $132,100 from her dad's IRA. That money went into a project that cost $135,000 (purchase price + rehab). So the IRS has Annie divide $132,100 by $135,000 to determine how much (what percentage) of the project was financed by debt. That will dictate how much of the profit is taxable. Let's take a look:

$132,100 ÷ $135,000 = .978519 or 97.85%

or for any other project Annie does:

Amount of Debt Incurred ÷ Total Amount of Project = UDFI

So now Annie takes her profit of $40,500 and multiplies it by her UDFI of 97.8519%:

Profit		UDFI		Taxable Amount
$40,500	x	97.8519%	=	$39,630

Annie now knows that $39,630 is TAXABLE. This is not the tax she pays, but it's the amount of the profit she must pay tax on. Out of her project, she pays UBIT on $39,630 and $370 is UBIT free.

Now we come back to the fact that a Roth is a trust. Because it's a trust, it pays tax at the trust tax rate. The trust tax is bracketed, just like income tax, but the maximum tax rate of 35% is reached at $11,200, so figure that any project worth doing, like Annie's, will be taxed at the maximum rate.

Figuring the tax on her taxable amount of $39,630, Annie finds she must pay UBIT of $12,846.

$40,500 profit - $12,846 UBIT = $27,654 profit net taxes.

Annie's Roth now has $27,654 plus her original $2,900. So in four months, Annie's Roth grew from $2,900 to $30,554. If Annie did three fix-n-flips in a year, one every four months, she reasonably could have $85,000 or more in 12 months!

Annie's project developed $27,654 off an investment of $2,900 in four months. Annie could have cut her costs considerably by putting $7,000 into the repairs of the house instead of $15,000, and also by finding a contractor that would have completed the job in half the time. Even with these drawbacks Annie's Roth grew considerably.

You might be wondering about reducing the UBIT that Annie pays. That certainly would increase her profitability, right? Let's take a look at eliminating UBIT.

In an IRA, Roth or Traditional, one of the ways of incurring UBIT is to use borrowed money. If you make a profit from a project using debt financing, you will pay UBIT. Let's assume Annie completes a project that uses exactly the same numbers, but without borrowing any money.

After a couple of years of similar deals, Annie now has the wherewithal to make cash purchases. Her Roth buys a house for $120,000 cash. She has enough money in her Roth to pay for all repairs. Using the same contractor (she's still making that mistake), she spends $15,000 to rehab the property. Once more Annie can only net $180,000 after transfer and broker's fees. The math is super simple this time:

Sale of House		Initial Investment		Gross Profit
$180,000	-	$135,000	=	$45,000

Now let's figure her UDFI:

Amount Borrowed		Cost of Project		UDFI
$0	÷	$135,000	=	0

Zero is a great number! If the UDFI is zero, what is the UBIT?

Profit		UDFI		Taxable Amount
$45,000	x	0	=	0

Isn't that great! Annie pays absolutely no UBIT! She should be very happy, right? But when Annie compares this project to her first project, she is at first puzzled, then upset. She finds she did much better on her first project than she thought. Here's what Annie found.

A good way to determine the value of a project, especially short term projects, is something called "Cash on Cash" return. If you buy something for $100 then sell it for $125, you have earned 25 dollars on your investment: you have a 25% cash on cash return. If you buy something for $100, sell it for $140, but you spend $15 in handling costs, you net $25. You still have a 25% cash on cash return. Cash-on-cash return can give you a quick measure of the value of an investment. Cash-on-cash return is only a fair indicator of longer term investment results, since you need to figure the time value of your money, opportunity costs and other factors when holding investments for over a year, but for short term investments, "Cash-on-Cash" return is an excellent way to judge.

Cash on Cash Return:

Profit		Initial Investment		Cash-on-Cash Return
$25	÷	$100	=	25%

When Annie figures her all cash project, it looks like this:

Profit		Initial Investment		Cash-on-Cash Return
$45,000	÷	$135,000	=	33%

That is a grand return. Annie's happy with it, and should be. Who wouldn't be happy with returns like that?

When she compares that to her first project, she is shocked, then amazed.

Profit		Initial Investment		Cash-on-Cash Return
$27,654	÷	$2,900	=	**953.6%**

Wait! Can that be right? 953.6%? Didn't she pay almost $13,000 in UBIT? Aren't the numbers on the projects almost the same? Is the math correct? The answers are yes, yes and yes.

Annie paid $12,846 in taxes, the numbers are almost the same, except for Annie's initial investment on both projects, and yes, the math is most absolutely correct.

The difference is that in the cash project, she invests $135,000, but in her first project she invests $2,900. How many $2,900 projects could she do with $135,000? Instead of doing one project, she could have done 45 projects with the same money. Her only problem is that she runs out of Dads to borrow from. This is a great example of how leverage affects your overall return. You've heard the term OPM (Other People's Money), and why it's so important to use it. Now you know.

And the UBIT tax? UBIT means you're making money. Trying to eliminate UBIT in a trust-taxed plan by reducing leverage seriously affects your overall return. In a real life situation, especially one involving bank lending, UDFI will rarely run higher than 60%. If that were the case here, Annie would pay only $7,480.50 in UBIT.

How many times can this been done in real life? A few. Dad only has to see the results of Annie's first project until he doesn't want to be a lender any more but wants to become an equity partner with her. Also in real life most people are never going to leverage that highly anyway. When dealing with banks, an IRA will probably be limited to a 60% loan to value, along with some other restrictions. We will talk about banks soon.

This was a pretty meaty chapter, so let's review the major concepts:

1. Any plan can do business with any other plan. Annie is restricted from doing business with her Dad's IRA, and Dad is restricted from doing business with Annie's Roth, but Annie's Roth can do business with Dad's traditional IRA. Remember, any plan can do business with any other plan.
2. Funds don't come OUT of an IRA to purchase property. All transactions occur WITHIN the IRA.
3. Titles to property are held in the plan's name. In this case Annie's custodian would be notified that she was going to buy a house. The house would be titled in her Roth's name. The title to the house would read something like this: "ABC Bank Trust as Custodian for Annie Investor Roth IRA".
4. There is a tax applied to IRAs called Unrelated Business Income Tax (UBIT). Although there are many ways to incur it in real estate transactions, one definite way to incur UBIT is to use debt to finance your project.

5. Debt financing results in a calculation called Unrelated Debt Financed Income (UDFI). Dividing the amount of the debt by the total cost of the project gives you a percentage. Multiplying that percentage by the amount of the profit gives the amount of profit that is taxable.
6. The taxable amount of profit determined by UDFI is taxed at the Trust Tax rate.
7. Leverage increases your cash on cash return considerably.
8. Reducing UBIT by reducing leverage reduces your cash on cash return.
9. It is counterproductive to reduce UBIT by reducing borrowing.
10. *BONUS 10. There is a super simple way to reduce or even eliminate UBIT. Keep reading!

Imagine the party Annie could have with just three Fix-n-Flips in a year. By earning even $80,000, Annie could have over $1 million in her Roth in 12 ½ years. Over $1 million! Bear in mind, she won't impact her time because she can't do any of the work herself. Consider also that Annie's million is completely income tax free. If Annie were 35, she could be a millionaire by 47. Being sharp, Annie knows she doesn't have to wait until 59 ½ to use that money, so she's planning ahead for some tax free income she can enjoy before retirement.

Wouldn't you like to party like Annie?

Points to Remember

1. People can be restricted. Plans never are.
2. Funds never come "out". "Out" is bad.
3. Unrelated Debt Financed Income is the basis of Unrelated Business Income Tax.
4. UDFI means Unrelated Debt Financed Income.
5. UBIT means Unrelated Business Income Tax.
6. Divide the amount borrowed by the total cost of the project to get UDFI.
7. Multiply profit by UDFI to find the taxable amount of income.
8. UBIT is very high and jumps to 35% after $10,000.
9. Leveraging increases our return..
10. Decreasing leverage to decrease UBIT is not productive.

9. Funding the Better Party

Even though Annie did an okay job on her house, she paid too much in improvements, her contractor took too long, and she paid 10% to Dad. Within the limits of her Roth, she did pretty well regardless. She could have done better with quicker turn around, and even though 10% seems like a high interest rate, it's really pretty reasonable for short term private cash.

Within the confines of a retirement plan, there are three sources of lending:

1. **Institutional Lending**: Non-Recourse Loans.
2. **Private Money Lending**: Individuals willing to make loans out of their own resources.
3. **Hard Money Lending**: Individuals or consortiums that lend at high rates.

There are a few banks that will lend money to retirement plans. They make Non-Recourse Loans. If you've never heard of these, don't feel bad. Most bankers haven't heard of them either. Let's investigate what a non-recourse loan is.

First I want to ask you, "Do you own your own home?" If it's yes, you probably said something like "Yeah, me and the bank" or "Yeah, I'm renting from the bank now." But either way, you and your bank have your names on the title, and you're basically in partnership with the bank. If you defaulted on your mortgage, could the bank take your house from you? The answer is "Yes! Of course they can." Can they come after you for more money even if they take the house? The answer is "Yes!" They call them 'deficiencies', and they include attorney's fees, transfer fees, court costs and other incidentals. In short, the bank has recourse against you.

If a bank were to lend to Annie's Roth for a property within her IRA, they would have NO recourse against her. If Annie had no income this year and a credit score of -450, her Roth would still qualify for a non-recourse loan. Annie's income, credit score, debt-to-income ratio: none of those can be considered by a lender making a non-recourse loan to a plan. Are you a real estate investor? Have you maxed out the number of homes you've purchased now becoming a high risk borrower? Your plan hasn't. Your IRA or 401K can borrow money from banks without that being a consideration. If the project goes south, the bank can only seize the property. They can't come after you for "deficiencies." Not only are you off limits, but with a Non-Recourse Loan the bank can't touch another penny in your plan. If you had $5 million in assets and went bust on a $500,000 property, the bank could only take the property, but would have to leave your $5 million untouched. Nice, huh?

The problem is that non-recourse loans are as rare as elephant feathers in Antartica. As of the writing of this book, there are two banks nationally that make non-recourse loans: First Western Federal and North American Savings Bank.

First Western Federal
402 Main Street
Rapid City, SD 57701
800-908-8845
www.myiralender.com

North American Saving Bank
12520 S. 71 Highway
Grandview, MO 64030
800-677-6272
www.nasb.com

Non-recourse lenders make loans only on income producing properties. In our example, if Annie had wanted to rent the property in her Roth, she could have done a refinance loan as long as she had a renter, a signed lease, and the house had some curb appeal. Although Annie can't personally guarantee the loan, her expertise as a landlord may be taken into consideration. Non-recourse lenders may have other qualifications as well.

In our example Annie used private money. "Private Money" is a term used in the real estate world to denote individuals that lend on various projects out of their own funds. These lenders lend at a rate higher than institutional lenders, but at a lower rate than 'hard money' lenders. Their terms are negotiable and can be very favorable to both parties. Interest rate, term, frequency of payment are but a few variables that can be negotiated in private money deals. Annie's Dad, for example, was very happy to get 10% on money that would have been more at risk in the market. Private money is definitely relationship borrowing, therefore must be cultivated over time. With private money, it is imperative that the borrower have a good name. Caution! There are many web sites touting private money, but they're actually promoting hard money.

Hard money lenders lend at rates of 15%+ and usually charge points. Points are an up front fee to make the loan and are a percentage of the total amount borrowed. Each point equals one percent of the loan amount. We won't go into the math here, but don't confuse the percentage of the points with the percent interest charged on the loan. A short term loan at 15% plus 3 points is not an 18% loan. It's closer to a 27% loan. The math is complicated and tricky to figure this, and part of it is determined by the length of the loan, so suffice it to say that hard money is that: HARD. Hard money should be used only on deals that have a payoff that warrants the cost of hard money, deals that are pre-sold so there are reduced carrying costs, or deals where the hard money is such a small percentage of the overall project that the high cost is negligible. Let's take a look.

An investor has a house he can purchase for $110,000, and has a buyer for it at $180,000 once it's fixed up. His drawback is that he only has $110,000 available to him, so he needs $10,000 for fixing. He finds a hard money lender that will charge 5 points and 20% for $10,000 for two months. That's right, 20% for two months is 120% per year APR. The five points or $500 he pays up front. His contracted sale goes through immediately after the fix-n-flip, so he receives his $180,000 net transfer fees. He now owes his hard money lender $12,000. Taken altogether, his acquisition costs are $122,500. His profit is now $57,500. Was it worth him paying the high interest rate? Of course. Could he carry that loan for long if his deal didn't go through? Not very well. Do investors borrow larger portions of their projects on hard money? Yes, they do. Can they lose their projects to a hard money lender? Yes, they can.

Not only do hard money lenders charge huge fees up front and very high rates of interest, they may include punitive terms on the loan as well. If a lender isn't paid in a specified period, they may take over the project, taking a first position on the mortgage. If our investor in this example had a punitive lender, he may have lost his house at the end of the second month if he can't cash out the hard money lender. These terms may be stringent, but if an investor needs cash badly enough and the deal is profitable and solid enough, hard money lenders are necessary and vital to the real estate business.

Now that you know the three types of lending available, you should understand that you don't need a huge amount of money in your retirement plan. You can have relatively small amounts then use OPM to maximize your profits.

But what about UBIT?

As we stated UBIT can be incurred by a variety of ways in IRAs. But wait! You've received another invitation to a better party! Buried in the IRS code is an invitation to the best party ever! This invitation was sent out on June 7th, 2001, known as the Economic Growth and Tax Relief and Reconciliation Act of 2001 (EGTRRA). Maybe your invitation got lost in the mail or maybe you didn't understand the invitation, but more likely, the guys on Wall Street threw it in the trash. This act allowed for the formation of the Solo 401K. Then in 2006, Congress sent you the invitation to the biggest blow-out bash ever. Even though the act passed in 2001, the Roth 401K wasn't enacted until January 1, 2006. Why is the Solo 401K so much better?

Read on! It's time to party hearty.

Points to Remember

1. Retirement plans can only receive Non-Recourse Loans from banks.
2. None of the participants' personal credit history is considered.
3. The participant cannot guarantee the loan.
4. Number of properties owned by the participant is never considered.
5. In a Non-Recourse Loan, the bank has recourse against the property on which it lends only.
6. None of the other assets in the retirement plan collateralize the loan.
7. Personal lending can be acquired from non-restricted individuals.
8. Rates on personal lending are negotiated.
9. Hard money must be used cautiously.
10. Hard money lenders charge high rates, up-front points and take the property if the loan defaults.

10. A Great Party

We need to understand the difference between all the parties we're invited to. The IRS has sent out so many invitations to all of us that we're really overwhelmed. Furthermore, most of these invitations have been sent to us via the people who stand to make the most money from our party: the caterers. Wall Street has poured millions upon billions of dollars into advertising and sales commissions to get you to allow them to cater your party. Think about it. When someone says "IRA" or "my 401K", what do you immediately think of? I'm willing to bet it's mutual funds. Some of you might think "annuity", and a few of you might think "CD at a bank." I'm going to also bet that few of you reading this have thought "Pizza parlor", "resort property", "angel investing", "fix-n-flips", "livestock", or "exporting hardwood from Brazil to Germany." I suggest you get a Kiplinger's magazine or the Wall Street Journal and count the ads for mutual funds, then count the ads for chickens, lumber, or foreclosed houses for retirement investing.

People ask all the time "Why haven't I heard of this before?" Now you know. No one's been telling you, and the people who can afford to tell you don't make any money by telling you, so they only tell you the information that's profitable to them. And the places for your money that give you total control and better returns can't afford to tell you.

So, not only are there a great parties being thrown, but they're parties that most don't know about. Once we realize that we can cater our own fête better than Wall Street, we still have to decide where to host our event.

We've seen that traditional IRAs and Roth IRAs can be wonderful tools for the self directed real estate investor, and we've also seen that they have an obscure and hidden tax. UBIT based on UDFI is not horrible, but it certainly affects the return we can garner within our plans. Although they haven't been addressed directly yet, Health Savings Accounts (HSAs) and Coverdell Educational Savings Accounts (CESAs) incur the same tax. We have seen that trying to reduce the tax by reducing leverage is counterproductive. Still, the tax reduces our real dollar return. Wouldn't it be great if we could somehow use leverage but not have to pay the UBIT based on UDFI?

Welcome to the best party around!

In 2001 Congress passed the Economic Growth and Tax Reform and Reconciliation Act (EGTRRA) allowing for Solo 401Ks. Up until the passage of EGGTRA 401Ks were expensive, cumbersome and difficult to administer. Congress enabled plans that were designed for small businesses where the compensated employees were also owners of the business. Prior to this act 401Ks were reserved for large corporations whose employee base justified the expense of instituting a large and cumbersome plan. Smaller businesses had the option of plans such as the Keogh or HR 10 plan, the SAR-SEP IRA (both now discontinued), the SEP-IRA and the SIMPLE IRA.

A small business owner could go crazy just trying to decide which plan would work best for his business. If a business owner wanted to minimize administrative costs, he would have chosen a SEP. If he wanted to have the flexibility of discretionary contributions, a profit sharing plan could have been the answer. Conversely, a young business owner with a long time horizon until retirement or one who wanted his employees to be able to fund part of their own retirement would have selected a SIMPLE or a 401(k) plan.

Confused? So are most Americans. This book doesn't attempt to address any of those plans. As a matter of fact, we want to encourage you to escape them. If you are a small business owner with employees, that is, employees that are not owners of your business, then you may be plunged into that morass without choice. If you are a small business owner that has recently downsized and got rid of your employees, or if you have always been self-employed without employees, you may have been limited to these choices before, thus you could have one of these plans hanging over your head. If you are a former employee, you may have money in such a plan or in an old 401K. Regardless of how you came to be a participant in these types of plans, this book is for you.

People have changed jobs enough recently that almost everyone has an old retirement plan hanging around out there. There is an old saying that "A confused mind will not make a decision." Consequently most people allow their old 401Ks, 403(B)s and other plans to drift without guidance.

Furthermore, most people are in hyper-managed, high cost, fee intensive mutual funds. Please read everything by Daniel R. Solin for a better treatment on this. I don't want to spend a lot of time on mutual funds and management fees, but I want to point something out to you.

When is 1% not 1%?

Take two 30 year olds. Like good managers of money, and exercising their best company options, they put some money every month into their companies' 401K. They get company matching funds for their efforts, which is great, bringing their total contribution to $200. Andy picks a fund he likes because of its inherent safety. Betty chooses a fund because it invests for better returns. Both funds have fees that exceed similar funds with similar results by 1%. That's right, just one percent.

Andy's fund would have grown at an average rate of 7%, but his return was reduced to 6% by that 1% difference. Betty's would have grown at 11% but returned only 10% for a similarly managed fund. Let's take a look at how they did. Each example shows the account balance at the end of the month with a constant return.

	Andy			Betty	
	7%	**6%**		**11%**	**10%**
Jan 2004	$201.13	$200.97		$201.75	$201.59
Feb 2004	$403.40	$402.93		$405.26	$404.80
ζ	ζ			ζ	ζ
Dec 2004	$2,490.06	$2,477.31		$2,540.72	$2,528.11
Dec 2005	$5,154.42	$5,103.25		$5,360.92	$5,309.03
ζ	ζ	ζ		ζ	ζ
Dec 2013	$34,403.78	$32,652.86		$42,485.95	$40,291.52
Dec 2023	$102,081.21	$91,129.15		$163,121.45	$144,797.35
Dec 2033	**$235,212.97**	**$195,851.29**		**$505,656.41**	**$415,858.54**
Lost Profit		$39,361.68			$89,797.87
Percentage Loss		**20.10%**			**21.59%**

The first two rows show how Andy's and Betty's funds grow by month. Each is in a fund that has a 1% higher fee than a fund achieving the same results, shown in the second column. Each column then jumps to year end. The next two lines show the growth at the end of two more years. They then both jump to the end of the decade, and then for every 10 years after that. At the end of 30 years Andy has missed out on $39,361.68 in earnings. He could have earned 20.1 % more in a lower cost fund returning the same results. Now look at Betty. Her 1% extra fee cost her $89,797.87 over her investing life. She lost approximately 21.6% of her profit. Not only did she lose more dollars, that 1% cost her a higher percentage of what she would have earned.

Party Island encourages you to take control of your future, your funds and your life starting right now. Welcome to the best party on the block. There is still one better party after this, but this new one is the most readily available to you. It's also the party you have to attend to get to the best results ever.

Welcome to the Solo 401K

Annie (remember Annie?) is a party girl. She loves to make her money grow and she knows how to do it really well. She knows she can beat Wall Street with a little study and some well applied principles. She loves being able to defer income taxes on her investments. She also realizes that her IRA, HSA, CESA can grow significantly better with real estate than with mutual funds.

Being as smart as she is, she is always on the lookout for something that will give her better returns and fewer hassles. Annie has discovered the Solo 401K. She is thrilled now that she has an even better vehicle for her retirement.

Since EGTRRA was passed in 2001, Solo (or Individual) 401Ks became available in 2002. Annie is thrilled to discover these are available to her. She establishes one for herself and promptly contributes $2,900 to it. That's not very much money, so she approaches her dad, making arrangements for her 401K to borrow from his IRA. She can do this because ANY PLAN can do business with ANY OTHER PLAN. She finds a $200,000 distressed property, then negotiates it down to $120,000 (sound familiar?), getting a 40% discount. Her 401K borrows $117,000 from her Dad's IRA, then borrows another $15,000 for the repairs done on the house. She spends too much on the rehab and she still hires the same contractor that takes four months instead of 6 – 8 weeks. It's still not a great time to sell a house, so she gets only $180,000 (net fees) for the property instead of the $200,000 she had hoped for. (You should be having a strong sense of déjà vu here.)

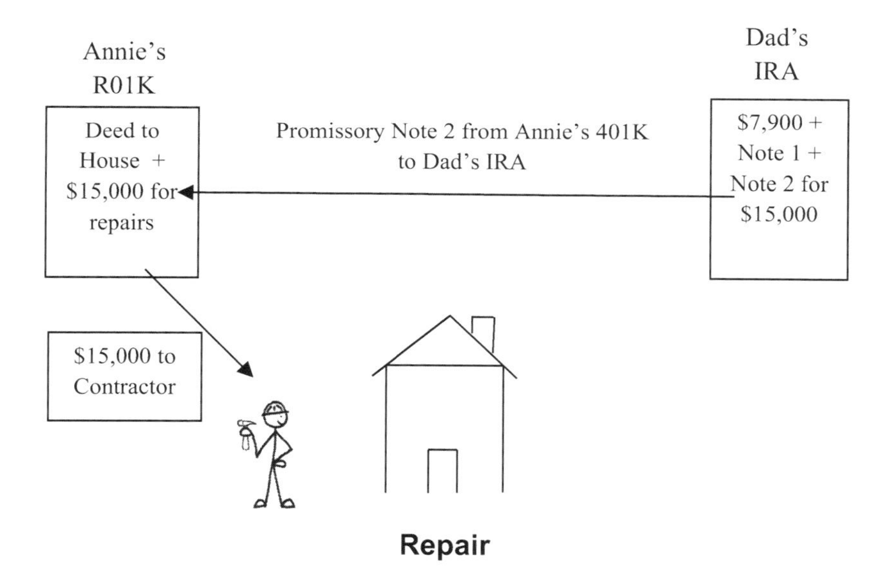

Once the repairs are completed, Annie sells the house. She nets the same amount as before and she pays back the same interest and principle to her father as she did before.

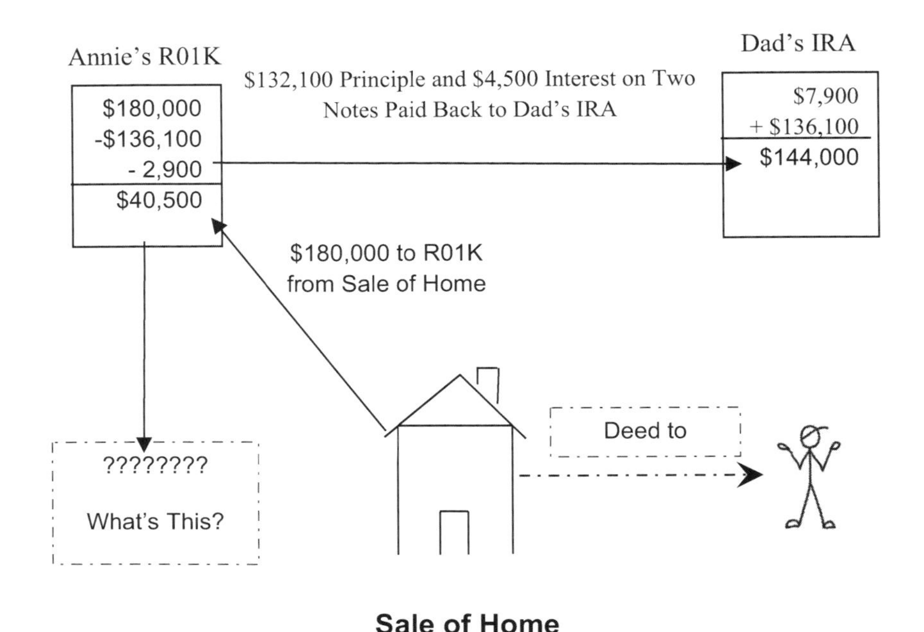

Sale of Home

Just so you don't have to turn back to the previous example of the transaction in the IRA, let's recap. Annie has $2,900 in her plan. She finds a distressed property she can buy for $120,000, which previously sold for $200,000. She borrows $117,100 from her dad at 10%. She hires a contractor that takes too long and encourages her to spend too much on the property. She borrows another $15,000 from her father also at 10%. The contractor takes 4 months instead of 6 – 8 weeks to finish the job. Annie sells the home for $180,000 instead of the $200,000 she had hoped for. She pays her contractor $15,000, then pays her father back the $132,100 she owes him plus $4,500.00 in interest. That leaves her $43,400 of which $2,900 is her original contribution. Annie now has

$40,500 that she must contend with.

Remembering her experience with her IRA, she knows she must calculate Unrelated Debt Financed Income (UDFI). Annie looks in the IRS rule book to find the factor for UDFI in 401Ks. She is delighted to find the number is ZERO! Zero, zip, zilch, nada! That's right, there is NO UDFI in 401Ks based on financing! This means her 401K gets to keep the entire $40,500 from the sale of her 401K's house. That's an extra $12,486.00 in her retirement for making exactly the same transaction in her 401K vs. her self directed IRA.

Now please understand, just because there is no UDFI doesn't mean there is no Unrelated Business Income Tax (UBIT). There can be UBIT generated in a 401K, but when it's generated, it's NEVER based on debt! There can be UBIT in a 401K, but you have to work hard to invoke it.

Remember: In a 401K there's never UDFI based on most leverage, which means that almost every type of leverage never incurs UBIT!

Remember also: You CAN incur UBIT through other means. That's right. UBIT still exists in a 401K. You have to work hard to incur it, but it exists. How can you run afoul of this tax?

1. Run a business. That's right, open a pizza parlor, sell T-shirts, own a shipping company, whatever. If you run a business from your 401K, you will pay 35% in taxes.
2. Owner financing. Yep, although I said leverage doesn't incur UDFI (and it doesn't), owner financing will incur UBIT. For some reason, the IRS really doesn't like owner financing at all. So don't buy something on land contract in your 401K, don't rent to own from the seller, don't give a partial payment for a property then pay the owner when the deal closes.

3. Allow the seller use of the property or retain any interest in the property after the sale: No lease backs, etc.
4. Allow the price to float: That is, give a partial down payment, then pay the difference of some future to-be-determined value to the seller.

If you avoid these, you will avoid UBIT, but there is a CAUTION SIGN ahead.

Do you recall point #1? It says that if you run a business out of your 401K, you will pay UBIT. Did you know that certain activities may not be a business until you do enough of them, then they become a business? To understand this, we need to turn our attention outside of 401Ks.

People have been doing fix-n-flips forever. During the runaway 2000s it was extremely lucrative, because once someone got a property looking attractive, it sold. This was fine if a person was a real estate professional (REP). It wasn't so nice if a person was a dealer. What's the difference between a dealer and a professional? Lots!

If you get classified as a real estate professional, the biggest warm fuzzy the IRS can give you arrives in your tax return. Remember when I talked about Limited Partnerships? Remember when I said the IRS got rid of most of those deductions? And remember when I said they got rid of most of them for most people? Well the people that kept them were Real Estate Professionals (REP). Being a real estate professional is an actual designation given by the IRS, that once achieved, allows the professional to write off passive losses against ordinary income. Why is that a big deal?

Tony works a full time job. Joanie, his wife is a stay at home mom. Although Tony works full time, he spends his weekends and some of his nights finding, negotiating, buying and maintaining rental properties.

Because of his full time position, it is impossible to convince the IRS that he qualifies as a REP. There are only two qualifications to becoming a REP:

1. More than half of the professional hours worked throughout the year must have been devoted to material participation in real estate activities.
2. More than 750 hours of material participation in real estate activities in the tax year being considered.

Because Tony works full time, the IRS won't believe that he works a another 2040 hours per year in real estate. Ah, but his wife Joanie, as a stay at home mom, can reasonably devote 14 ½ hours per week to their rental properties. That exceeds the 750 hours that's necessary for the REP designation, and since she has no other employment, this could constitute 100% of her professional hours. That's great because only one person in a marriage needs to be a REP to get the benefits. And what are the benefits?

Tony owns five properties each worth $250,000 for a total of $1,250,000. The land itself never depreciates, but the buildings do, so at the end of the year, Tony figures his depreciation at $28,525. He collects $1,300 a month rent on each property, but must pay property taxes, interest and insurance on all of them. A hail storm necessitates new roofs on all his structures. After all his maintenance and operating expenses, Tony has net income of $13,800. His depreciation is $28,525, so it completely eliminates any taxable income from his property, but it leaves $14,725 in unused depreciation. If he's a dealer, that unused depreciation sits on the shelf until the property is sold. If he or his wife is designated a real estate professional, Tony can deduct that $14,725 from his income, even if his income is over $250,000. Pretty neat, huh?

Even if Tony or his wife have the REP designation, they can lose it by performing more than four fix-n-flips a year. Yep, if they sell four houses in a year that they've held for less than 366 days, then the IRS pulls their REP status, all the wonderful use of depreciation goes away, and it may become difficult to get it back.

And how does the IRS determine if you should lose your REP designation? They look at your intent.

What? How does someone measure intent? There's a story about intent that seems to be appropriate here. Two men jump off a bridge into a river. One is a fool and one is a hero. The first man jumped off to commit suicide and the second man jumped to save him. There previously had been a law passed to stop kids from diving and bungee jumping off this bridge, making jumping and diving illegal, so both men were charged with breaking the law. So how does the IRS know what your intent is? Here are their criteria.

- Purpose for acquiring, holding and selling the property
- Number, frequency and continuity of sales
- Duration of ownership
- Time and effort expended by the taxpayer in promoting sales
- Use of brokers
- Extent of improvements and subdivision made to facilitate sales
- Ordinary business of the taxpayer
- Extent and value of the taxpayer's real estate holdings

- Extent and nature of the transactions involved
- Amount of income from sales as compared with the taxpayer's other sources of income
- Desire to liquidate landholdings unexpectedly obtained
- Overall reluctance to sell the property
- Amount of advertising
- Use of a business office for sales
- Control over any sales representatives

Nice, huh? So really it boils down to the auditor who's looking at your history of investing and selling. The main issue appears to be "Number, frequency and continuity of sales". Although it's a moving target, and can vary from IRS agent to IRS agent, it seems that four is the magic number.

Four seems to be the magic number outside, but inside your 401K the magic number is "3". If you are a fix-n-flipper outside your 401K and you flip more than four houses, you will lose many of the tax advantages inherent to real estate. If you flip more the three houses inside your 401K, you will incur UBIT, that is, you have gone from "investing" to "running a business". To make matters even more confusing, you could be considered a dealer on some of your flips and not on others. Conversely, the house that makes you a dealer may disqualify all the other houses so that you will now incur UBIT on all of them, again, depending on the IRS agent you draw.

Now if you own property for income in your 401K, you can own a million houses. There is no limit to rental properties for investment, but for short term flips, that is, houses owned for less than a year, your limit is three. Consider though that a well managed fix-n-flip can garner anywhere from $25,000 to $40,000 in profit. If a person were to average $30,000 per flip that would mean your 401K could grow by $90,000 per year. Then when those funds weren't actively tied up in houses, they could be invested elsewhere.

These are not unreasonable figures. You may be asking yourself questions such as: "Where can I buy houses like that?" or maybe "Sure, that sounds good on paper, but can it be done in real life?"

I gave my presentation one night to a father, son and some of their friends. The young man, in his late 20s, told me he makes $30,000 per flip on the houses he's done. He does most of the work himself, so even if he had to keep hands-off due to his 401K restrictions, his fix-n-flip would garner him about $25,000 per house. At 3 per year, his 401K could grow at $75,000 per year, and all he would have to do is shop for the property. At the time of this writing, it's 2011 in Sun Prairie, Wisconsin. This was when professionals were saying "the real estate market is really bad", and "now is not the time to flip, like it was a couple of years ago." Oh, and "nobody can get a loan right now." All these statements have been used to describe the current real estate condition, yet this young man has been making $30,000 per house.

So to recap, a 401K is immensely superior to an IRA because a person gets to retain all the Unrelated Business Income Tax (UBIT) that normally would have disappeared out of the IRA on the same transaction. Let's compare.

	Annie's IRA	Annie's 401K
Profit	$40,500	$40,500
UDFI	97.85%	0%
Taxable Income	$39,630	$0
UBIT Bracket	35%	N/A
UBIT Due	$12,846	$0
Profit Net UBIT	$27,654	$40,500

Now if you remember in the discussion of self directed IRAs, we said trying to avoid UBIT by paying cash was counter-productive. That still remains true for IRAs. But we can avoid UBIT simply by opening a Solo 401K. That puts anywhere from 30 – 50% more profit in our pockets on the same investment.

So, reason number 1 that 401Ks outshine IRAs: NO UDFI and limited UBIT!

Ok, so let's go back to Chapter 6, when we were talking about restricted transactions. The same rules apply to your 401K: you may not sell to, nor buy from, lend to nor borrow from, make non-cash contributions to nor garner secondary benefits from your 401K (with one exception).

That exception is called a Participant Loan! A participant loan is a specific attribute of a 401K. It is well defined and does not fall under any of the other rules regarding restricted transactions. To keep this straight, remember a PARTICIPANT LOAN is never restricted, but if it's any other kind of loan, it IS restricted.

The loan that Annie's Dad's IRA made to her Roth has terms, interest and an amount negotiated between him and Annie. That is NOT a participant loan. If Annie had enough money in her 401K, she could strike a promissory note like that with anyone in the world, except herself, her dad and any other restricted person. Those types of loans are restricted.

So what is a participant loan? And why is it not restricted?

The second question is the easiest to answer: Participant loans aren't restricted because congress says they aren't. It's part of the law governing 401Ks. Participant loans have been available as a part of 401K plans since their institution. If you've worked for a corporation that offered a 401K, you may be aware that they offered participant loans. The rules for offering loans are malleable and can be chosen by the employer cafeteria style. The availability of participant loans lay along a continuum that the employer can choose from.

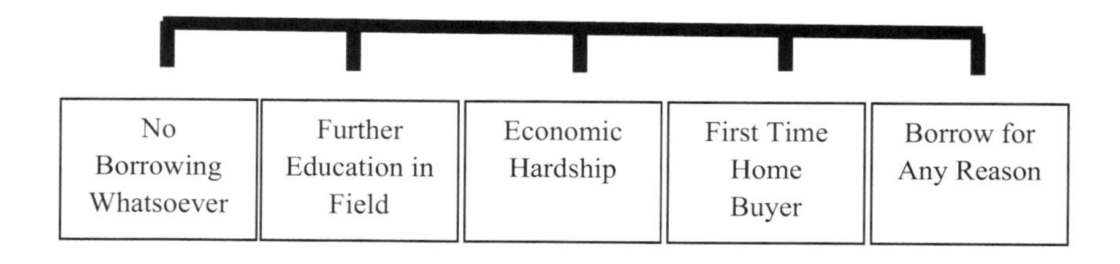

I have seen plans that are completely restrictive and don't allow any borrowing. Most plans allow some means of getting participant loans, usually for education related to employment, economic hardship, first time home buying status, or other qualifications determined by the employer. The employer may allow one of these or some or all. Almost no employers allow the option for participant loans for any reason. This is usually a stipulation imposed by the financial institution servicing the corporate 401K, because they don't want to lose the assets under management and the fees they garner from those assets. It's often touted as "protecting the retirement of the employee" and supposedly it does this, but without a doubt, restricting the availability of loans helps the broker and the mutual fund company as much or more than it does the employee.

Annie is delighted to find that as the sponsor of her own 401K, she gets to decide how she will make participant loans to herself. Should she restrict herself entirely from having access to her own money? Should she put some kind of stipulation on her own borrowing? Or should she allow herself complete access to this provision?

Annie has decided to treat herself the very best she can, so she is going to allow herself to use the participant loan provision for any reason she sees fit. And so can you! When you establish your Solo 401K, you can give yourself the same privilege. Let's look at a participant loan to see why they're so special.

A loan has three parts: principle, interest and term. A participant loan defines these as follows:

Principle: 50% of your 401K value up to $50,000.

Interest: A good rule of thumb is prime + 1%. You can set the rate below prime, and you can set the rate up to prime + 3%, but there are risks in doing so. If the IRS determines your loan rate is too low, they'll class the loan as a distribution. If you set the rate too high, they'll interpret the loan as a concealed contribution, that is, a way to contribute more to your 401K than the contribution limit allows. Prime + 1% will always keep you in good graces with Uncle IRS.

Term: The term can be any term up to a maximum of five years. The payments may be monthly or quarterly as long as equal payments are made. Even though the rule stipulates equal payments, the loan may be prepaid as long as it's paid off in its entirety.

What does this mean for a participant? Let's take a look at Annie. She's direct-transferred or invested enough in her 401K to accumulate $100,000. By the terms defined in 401K rules, she can borrow up to $50,000 as a PARTICIPANT LOAN. If that money had stayed in her IRA, NONE of that $50,000 would be available to her. But because she has chosen to establish a solo 401K, she now has access to $50,000 of her retirement money.

Annie chooses Prime + 1 as her interest rate. As of the writing of this book, her loan rate would be 4.25%. Annie chooses 5 years as her term. Calculating the payments on the loan, her monthly payments back to her 401K would be $926.48, and her interest that she paid herself the first year would be $1,947.74. If she chose quarterly payments, her payments would be $2,788.23 and her first year interest would be $1,980.10. But Annie discovers something really exciting about this loan.

If Annie were to use this loan as a down payment on her personal residence, or to fix or repair her own home, her loan would just be a loan that she has to pay off. But, and this is a big but, if she were to use that loan for an investment or any other business purpose, she could write off the interest on that loan!

That's right, since interest on a loan is a legitimate business deduction, Annie can write off the interest she's paying to HER OWN 401K, as long as the loan is not for personal use! That means you can too!

Think of the implications. You may have old IRAs and old 401Ks hanging around. If they were to be rolled into a solo 401K for yourself, you could borrow the money from those funds, invest it, pay the loan back with interest, keep the profit in your own pocket, and WRITE OFF THE INTEREST YOU PAY YOURSELF!

Is that good or great?

Two caveats on participant loans. You may only take one loan at a time. If you take a participant loan on Monday for $20,000 out of the $50,000 you have available to you, and the following Monday a person shows up with a fantastic opportunity that needs $30,000, you may not generate a second loan. You would have to pay back the $20,000, then borrow the $50,000 to allow you to meet both needs.

The second precaution you need to take is that your payments, whether you choose monthly or quarterly, must be made on time and in equal amounts. There are no partial prepayments. You can't take your tax return and dump some of it against the loan you have outstanding. You may, however, pay off the loan entirely at any point with no pre-payment penalty.

So there are two fantastic advantages of a Solo 401K over a self directed IRA: 1.) NO UDFI! and 2.) Participant loans that allow you to pay yourself with the ability to deduct the interest if used correctly!

But Annie has discovered something that truly delights her. There is NO CUSTODIAN. Annie is her own trustee under the 401K plan. She is in charge of the filings, she is in charge of the investments, she is in charge of the timing, she is in complete charge of her future and her funds. Annie will establish two accounts for her Solo 401K immediately. She will establish a checking and a savings account. If an opportunity presents itself, Annie can write a check as the trustee for her 401K without having to send a letter of intent or any other filings with some custodian somewhere. Not only can Annie better control her investments, there are NO custodial fees with a 401K. That's more money for Annie's retirement.

The best advantage of the 401K is that there are no income limits for contributions. If Annie had stuck with her IRA or Roth, the income limits differ for each type of account, and the limits vary as to her filing status (single, married filing jointly, married filing separately, single head of household). This makes determining your income limits with IRAs very confusing. Some income limits are very punitive, restricting your ability to save for your own future. With the Solo 401K Annie looks up the income limits and WOW she finds there are none! Married, single, joint, separate, all that goes away with the 401K. The confusion disappears when she understands THERE ARE NO INCOME LIMITS!

Although the reporting procedure is slightly more complicated for a 401K, it is not overwhelming.

One drawback to the 401K is the imposition of Required Minimum Distributions. Of course, traditional IRAs have these as well, and the only plan that is not subject to them is the Roth IRA.

Annie will set up a Roth IRA to act as her "Get Out of Jail Free" card, which we'll discover later.

Annie has a heck of a party going now. She has her money working for her about as well as she can in the traditional side of retirement planning. She has full control of her money; she can borrow against her retirement, then deduct the interest if used properly; she doesn't have to worry about earning too much or changing filing status affecting her ability to contribute; and her investments are more profitable because she isn't saddled with UDFI!

The only thing Annie could do better, is to move to Party Island. Remember we talked about those off-shore tax havens? And how we didn't need to move off shore to take advantage of them? Annie's about to discover Party Island buried in the IRS Tax Code. She's already part of the way there, since she's established her Solo 401K.

Before we move to the island, let's take a look at what we've learned.

Solo 401K	**Traditional IRA**
Advantages	**Disadvantages**
You're your own Trustee	Custodian Required
No Custodial Fees	Custodial Fees, usually based on amount of assets
No UDFI	UDFI with resulting UBIT
Investments More Profitable	Return lower due to UBIT
Participant Loans	No Loans EVER to IRA owners
Tax Deductible Interest on loans for business use	Not Available
No Income Limits	Limits vary with income and filing status
Disadvantages	**Advantages**
More Reporting Required	Reporting done by Custodian

Clearly, the Solo 401K gives a person more freedom and self determination, as well as the opportunity for greater profits. Party on dude!

Points to Remember

1. 401Ks are far superior to IRAs.
2. There are no custodial fees
3. Even at 1%, custodial fees can be costly.
4. It's difficult to incur UBIT in a 401K.
5. Investments are 30% - 50% more profitable in a 401K because of the lower incidence of UBIT.
6. You can borrow your own money from the 401K.
7. Your money is completely hands-off in an IRA.
8. You can deduct the interest you pay your own 401K if the loan is used for business purposes.
9. Roth provision of the 401K incurs no UBIT or UDFI in most cases.
10. No income limits on contributions.

11. Welcome to Party Island

I think most of you will agree that getting to an island is slightly more difficult than getting anywhere on shore. This analogy holds true for establishing our Solo 401Ks to maximum advantage. Consider the following diagram.

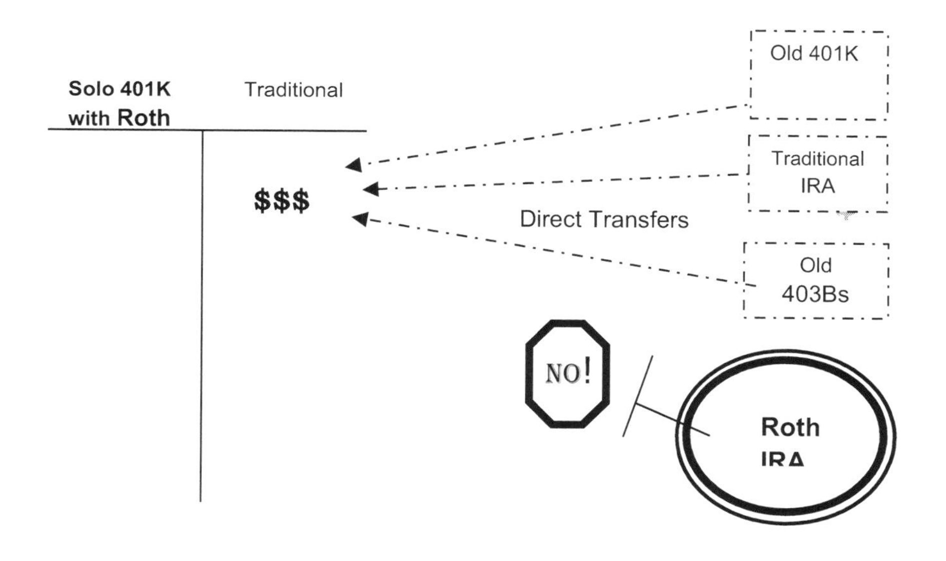

You can see from this diagram that transferring funds from old 401Ks, Traditional IRAs, and old TSAs (403Bs) can be done easily. If done as a direct transfer from the old accounts to the new Solo 401K, there are no tax consequences. There is also a rollover, which has specific uses and should be used cautiously. Many people use the words "rollover" and "transfer" interchangeably, but as Mark Twain said, "The difference between the right word and almost the right word is like the difference between lightning and the lightning bug." If you mean to do a transfer, and you do a rollover instead, you might feel as though you've been struck by lightning. A transfer directly exchanges funds between two custodians, a custodian and a trustee, or two trustees, thus incurs no taxes.

In a rollover, the participant takes possession of the money for up to 60 days, then deposits it in the new plan. If a person takes a rollover from a 401K, say, from a previous employer, the trustee of the old 401K is required by law to withhold 20% of the rollover. That means the participant will be 20% shy on their new deposit and will pay tax and penalties as though it were a lump sum distribution. There's usually no need for it and it's fraught with danger.

In Annie's example, she can transfer money from her old 401K, the Traditional IRA she's established, and many other retirement accounts as long as she's left employment from the sponsor of the plan. Once the transfer has taken place, she has full control of the funds, acts as her own trustee, can borrow some of the money through participant loans, and will avoid paying UDFI on most leveraged transactions. One added advantage not discussed earlier is that Annie can now trade stocks on margin in her 401K if she chooses to do so. That transaction is prohibited under the other plans.

Also notice that the Roth IRA may not be rolled over to the Roth Provision of the Solo 401K. Why is this? Only congress and the IRS know for sure, but it cannot be done.

So where is this Party Island? Party Island exists in the Roth Provisions of the Solo 401K. Why is it an island? Because it's hard to get to. But, MAN, once you're there, fantastic things can happen!

Party Island exists in the Roth Provisions of the Solo 401K. You party better than the Roth IRA and you party a lot better than the Traditional IRA or 401K. And it's better than a tax free haven offshore because your money is at your fingertips with your full control. But all your profits, whether small or sizable remain completely and totally income tax free.

The Roth Provisions of the Solo 401K is just too long to write all the time, so we'll christen it the R01K. Party Island will henceforth be known as the R01K. The less popular and less useful Traditional Provision will be known as a T01K.

First let's take a look at the tax consequences of saving money in a Traditional IRA and the Traditional side of the 401K (T01K). I want you to consider this (Caution – more math coming): If you are in the 33% tax bracket, that is, you are earning between $212,300 - $379,150 per year, and you deposit $15,000 into your 401K, you will garner a tax deduction worth $5,000 to you. If, however, you're like the majority of us, your tax deduction will amount to $4,200 or less. Now let's consider what can happen.

We've seen that Annie can use leverage to make amounts like that grow considerably, WITHOUT ANY FURTHER CONTRIBUTIONS! So consider that Annie could easily grow her traditional account to $1,000,000 over her lifetime. When Annie retires, she wants access to her money and begins to draw it out. When Annie turns 70 ½ she MUST draw it out whether she wants to or not. This is because both TIRA's and T01Ks have Required Minimum Distributions (RMD). Uncle Sam's plan for you is to have you take your money out, tax it, and then have you spend it. The most operative part of that plan is: TAX IT.

If Annie has $1,000,000 in her traditional plans at 70, and she takes her distributions according to the IRS schedule of RMDs, Annie will wind up in a 28% tax bracket. She will incur a tax liability of $280,000. Now think about this. The government gave her a tax break of $5,000, but she incurs a tax liability of $280,000. Is this a fair trade? If this seems appealing to you, I will make you that deal right now. I'll give you $5,000 today, and when you retire in 20 – 30 years, you pay me $280,000. This may cause many of you to start thinking about contacting your broker to do an IRA to Roth conversion. DON'T. Read the rest of the book, then decide what you want to do. There may be a better alternative.

Regardless of that, we can see that in the traditional accounts, Uncle IRS stands waiting for us to age to the point that we are just tax wells waiting to be drawn from. So let's compare our first two "tax advantaged" accounts

Using Annie's example of a moderately successful fix-n-flip, let's see how our accounts compare.

	Average Gross Profit	UBIT Paid	Profit Net UBIT	Homes per $1,000,000	Distribution Tax Liability
T01K	$40,500	$0	$40,500	25	$280,000
TIRA	$40,500	$12,346	$27,654	36	$280,000

To steer clear of any negative tax effects that could be imposed by the IRS, Annie limits her transactions inside her plans to three fix-n-flips per year. This means she becomes a millionaire in 8 years with her 401K vs. 12 years in her TIRA. If Annie is 35, she's a millionaire by age 43 instead of age 47. What happens in the next 12 years? Doing what she's been doing consistently, Annie accumulates $3 million in her T01K in the time it took her to do $2 million in her TIRA. But even then, she incurs a $280,000 tax liability for every $1M she accumulates.

Now let's compare these transactions occurring in her available Roths. First we'll contrast a Roth IRA with the traditional accounts.

	Average Gross Profit	UBIT Paid	Profit Net UBIT	Homes per $1,000,000	Distribution Tax Liability
Roth IRA	$40,500	$12,346	$27,654	36	$0
T401K	$40,500	$0	$40,500	25	$280,000
TIRA	$40,500	$12,346	$27,654	36	$280,000

Of course, I can hear some of you saying "Yes, but she doesn't get any deduction for her contribution." So what? You must be the same person who thinks taking $5,000 from me today to incur a $280,000 payment back to me in the future is a good deal.

Think about this. A married couple filing jointly will be in a 25% tax bracket earning about $70,000. If they have kids, it's highly unlikely that they'll be able to sock away $15,000 into their 401K. They simply can't afford the reduction in income. So let's say they put $5,000 into a traditional IRA for the tax break. They will receive a tax break of $1,250. If they put same amount into their Roth, they'll receive no tax break whatsoever. If they invest using leveraged real estate like Annie, they'll be $280,000 richer when they retire on the $1,000,000 accumulated in their Roth IRA. Which would be better for them: to have $1,000,000 tax free at their disposal, or to retire on $720,000 after taxes?

Now let's see what happens on Party Island. Annie is going to conduct all the same transactions in her Roth 401K that she's been conducting in her other accounts. Let's see how that compares.

	Average Gross Profit	UBIT Paid	Profit Net UBIT	Homes per $1,000,000	Distribution Tax Liability
Roth 401K	$40,500	$0	$40,500	25	$0
Roth IRA	$40,500	$12,346	$27,654	36	$0
T401K	$40,500	$0	$40,500	25	$280,000
TIRA	$40,500	$12,346	$27,654	36	$280,000

So the choice should be very simple. Pick the row with the most zeroes in it. By investing in the Roth 401K, Annie incurs the lowest tax on each transaction, and eliminates any tax liability at the end of her investing career. Isn't that worth the paltry write-off she's giving up? As one person said, "Your money goes to heaven" in an R01K. But the tax savings are only the beginning of the party. It gets so much better that it seems almost unreal.

Annie is a little impatient. She is accumulating wealth rapidly and as a 35 year old, considers 59 ½ to be a long way off. She would love to have some of her tax free money now. She can always take out her initial contribution without penalty, as long as she does it after 5 years, but that's not really tax free money. She's already paid the taxes on her contribution. So let's see what happens when she's 40. Annie has consistently done three fix-n-flips per year in her Roth 401K. After five years she has amassed $607,000 in her 401K. She would like to get at some of that, but there is no way to withdraw it without complications from her 401K.

But Annie has a "Get Out of Jail Free" card. It's called a Roth IRA. When she was 35, she opened a small Roth at a bank for some minimal amount. Now that she's 40, this Roth no longer has the 5 year restriction on it. If you remember our earlier diagram, we said that it's not possible to transfer out of a Roth to a 401K. But the good news is, it's possible to transfer INTO a Roth IRA.

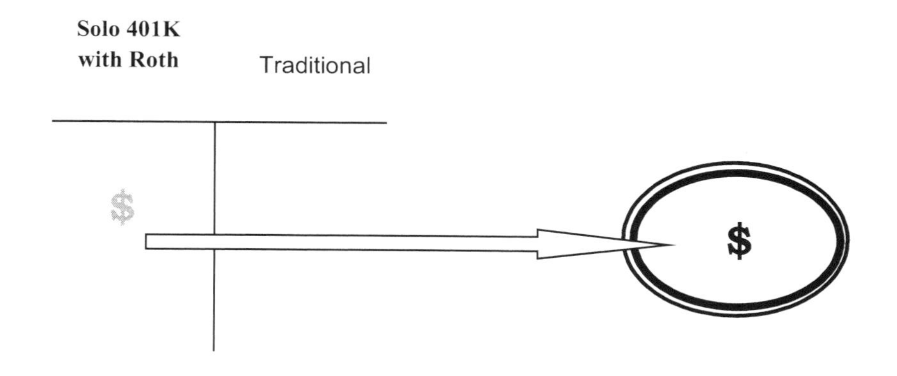

Annie knows another wonderful thing about Solo 401Ks – there's a back door on them! There's actually a back door on every 401K, but for most of them they are nailed, bolted and welded shut. The backdoor we're talking about is called an In-Service Distribution. It is an option that can be instituted with 401Ks but almost never are. Why? Because the financial firm that operates the 401K for the employer doesn't want the employees taking money out of the plan at any time. The financial institution gets a cut of all the assets under management, so under no circumstances does that firm want to see money going away. This is one of the main reasons that there are restrictions on participant loans as well.

But since Annie manages her own 401K, she's going to allow herself to transfer out of it at any time. Bear in mind that transferring out of it is NOT taking a distribution. It merely means that she could now transfer it to a Roth IRA without having to die, become disabled, or turn 59 ½. Annie loves the In-Service Distribution because it allows her to set up something called a 72t distribution.

Retire Early and Retire Often on Party Island

RothIRAs are eligible to set up a 72t distribution. Although technically a 401K could set up a 72t, setting one up freezes the account, which you would never want to do to your 401K. Therefore it's easier to have set up a Roth IRA to transfer into when necessary.

Also known as a SEPP, which stands for Substantially Equal Periodic Payments, a 72t distribution is calculated using the participant's life expectancy, the amount of the principle being distributed and some "reasonable" interest rate. If you're wondering what reasonable is, the IRS will be glad to tell you. The rate the IRS imposes as reasonable is "*not more than 120 percent of the federal mid-term rate (determined in accordance with 1274(d) for either of the two months immediately preceding the month in which the distribution begins).*" So basically the IRS says you must take the last two months of mid term bonds issued, multiply that by 1.2, then choose a rate equal to or less than that. So if the mid-term rate for government bonds last month was 3%, you would multiply that by 1.2 to get 3.6%. You could then use 3.6% or less to calculate your payments. Confused? Yep, me too.

Regardless, you can determine an annual distribution based on your age, amount to be distributed and a reasonable interest rate. If Annie had $607,000 in her Roth 401K, she could transfer $300,000 to her Roth IRA that is now five years old. Once she transfers her $300,000, Annie splits some of that off to another Roth IRA. Notice I didn't say "new". A new Roth would have to start the five year restriction all over again. By splitting her existing Roth to another Roth, this second Roth is considered to have fulfilled the five year restriction requirement. So now Annie has her 401K, her original Roth now worth $300,000, and her additional Roth seeded from her original. Why does she want another Roth?

Once a 72t distribution has begun, the Roth becomes frozen. No more contributions may be made to it, and the payments established must be continued unchanged. Once Annie determines how much she can withdraw annually, regardless of the change in value of the Roth, those payments must continue as established. If Annie would like more of her R01K retirement in the future, she would have to have another Roth to establish a 72t. Planning ahead, she duplicates her existing Roth IRA to allow her to do just that.

So at age 40, Annie uses her In-Service Distribution to transfer some of her R01K money to her Roth IRA. Using the amortization method Annie finds she can take a $12,296 tax and penalty-free distribution from her Roth.

She now has $12,296 coming to her every year. The drawback on this is that once she starts taking that distribution, she MUST continue it until age 59 ½. That's right, she MUST take her $12,296 TAX FREE money whether she wants it or not.

Now bear in mind that the distribution must continue until age 59 ½ and that she can no longer make contributions to her Roth. She can, however, continue to invest and co-invest her Roth IRA with her R01K. The drawback is that she will incur UBIT in her Roth IRA, but that is the trade off she must make for using her money early.

A couple of years later, Annie decides she needs more tax free income. She establishes another 72t distribution in her duplicate Roth IRA, and because she's two years older, she can now take a distribution of $12,577. This additional distribution gives her a tax free income of $25,873. Ask yourself, would an additional $25 - $26,000 TAX FREE income make a difference in your life?

There are actually three methods of establishing a 72t from a Roth but the complexity of comparing them goes beyond the scope of this book. Check out "Retire Early and Retire Often on Party Island" for a more thorough understanding of this topic.

Okay, so now we have a better picture of what Party Island looks like. It looks like this:

- No UDFI (if done correctly)
- Ability to Borrow Retirement Funds through Participant Loans
- Deductibily of Interest on Participant Loans if Used for Business Purposes
- Access to Tax Free Income before 59 ½
- No Tax Liability at retirement

We have a pretty good party started, but we haven't really kicked off the best part of the proceedings yet. This is where the clown shows up with balloon animals, where the girl jumps out of the cake, where all the free gifts are handed out to the attendees.

I want you to put this book down for a few seconds. Close your eyes. Remember, don't imagine, but remember the nicest place you've ever been in your travels. Were you skiing? Boating? Golfing? Was it warm and balmy? Cold and bracing? Were you fishing? Hunting? Shopping? Snow boarding? Maybe there are two spots that you like equally? One for summer activities and one for winter activities. It could even be somewhere out of the country. Mexico? Belize? Brazil? Bali? Italy? Canada? Take few seconds, heck, take a minute and really get the feel of where you'd like to spend a lot of time.

Are you back now? Great! Let's see what Annie chose. She chose some land down on the Kenai Peninsula in Alaska and some beach front property outside of Biloxi, Mississippi. She's a smart girl, so she's always a bargain hunter. She has a couple of look outs in these areas that watch for divorces, estate sales and foreclosures for properties that could be bought at a discount. As they become available, she buys them in her Roth 401K. Now remembering her restrictions, Annie knows that any property owned in her 401K is off-limits to her. She can have it managed, she can watch its cash flow pour into her Roth provision, she can drive by it to see how it's being maintained, but she can't use it in any way. Really. She is completely restricted.

That being said, she watches these properties increase in value while making a nice income for herself as she makes her way to retirement. Then a magical thing happens to Annie.

She turns 59 ½.

When she turns 59 ½ all her distributions from her R01K become tax and penalty free! Bear in mind, that's ALL her distributions. And Annie knows something else about distributions that most brokers, bankers and insurance people don't know.

Distributions don't have to be taken as cash.

That's right. There's no law, legislation, rule or requirement that says distributions must be taken as cash. Annie has known this and has been planning on it since her investing began. The day she turns 59 ½ her trustee of her 401K (that's Annie) deeds the Alaska property and the Biloxi property to the plan participant (that's Annie), and now Annie owns two properties that she dearly loves. She now owns personally the two places she wants to spend her free time, to spend her retirement or to spend time with her kids and grandkids whenever she wants. There would be transfer fees, of course. She would have to pay the local authorities to retitle the properties, but there would be NO FEDERAL INCOME TAX.

This type of distribution is called Payment In Kind, or PIK. PIK distributions are very powerful and can apply to just about anything you can imagine. I'm from southwest Wisconsin, so if you look at a map you'll see there is a dearth of oceans here. Because of that I would have never thought of the following scenario. One of my clients is from Rhode Island, and if you look at a map you'll see that they have a lot of ocean there. When I explained PIK distributions to him, he said "What about my yacht?" I had a moment of clarity when it dawned on me "Of course his yacht!" Why not? His R01K could buy a yacht and lease it to some company to do whatever that earns income. The income from this arrangement could pay for the yacht, then when he turns 59 ½ he would own his yacht free and clear as a PIK distribution to himself out of his R01K.

Now that's a party! And it's on a tax free paradise called an R01K. So there must be a hitch somewhere, right? If it sounds too good to be true, it must be, right? There's got to be a skunk in the wood pile somewhere. There are two speed bumps on our way to Party Island. Or more precisely, there are two speed bumps: one onto Party Island and one leaving Party Island. Both must be taken into consideration, but both are easily overcome.

The speed bump on the way to Party Island: All contributions must be new money. Unless you are rolling over an existing 401K with Roth provisions, there is no way to get money into the R01K except through new contributions. Because the Roth provision was made permanent only in 2006, there are few people that have 401K / Roth money at this time. So if you are one of the lucky ones to have made contributions to the Roth side of your corporate 401K, you may transfer directly to your R01K, otherwise you're limited to new money.

The speed bump on the way off of Party Island: Required Minimum Distributions. When you turn 70 you must start taking your very valuable money out of your R01K. The same penalties apply as a T01K or TIRA if you don't.

But let's take a look at the speed bump on the way in. Unless you have begun to contribute to an R01K, there are no conversions from Traditional Plans into an R01K, there are no transfers or rollovers into an R01K, the only way in is to use new money. You must have earned income (remember, that's no rent, gambling winnings, inheritance, dividends, interest, long term capital gains, insurance proceeds, etc.) So where can this money come from?

This money must come from your business. If you'll recall, we likened the business owner to the people at the party who were having a great time. If you are not a business owner, you need to become one. I don't care what you do, as long as it's a business. What's a business? Any legal activity recognized by your state. This book is specifically aimed at people who want to conduct real estate transactions as their business, but any business will do. Sell Mary Kay. Give Tupperware parties. Sign up to represent Shaklee. There are 100s of home marketing businesses that are available to you at your fingertips. Have a hobby? Make it a business. Babysit. Mow your neighbors' lawn. Take kids on educational field trips. Defrag a computer, but DO SOMETHING.

If you are currently employed by a firm that's not your own, you are probably receiving W2 income. That income cannot become a contribution to your R401K. If you have opened a legitimate business, then you can contribute up to 100% of your income or $16,500 whichever is less. You can adjust that minimum to $22,000 if you are over 50. Now please note, your current income, if it's W2 income from a firm that's not your own CANNOT be contributed to your Solo 401K.

Setting up the necessary entities lies beyond the scope of this book, but if you're serious about investing in real estate or in other non-Wall Street investments, there are simple strategies for you to implement that allow you to seed your R01K. Check out "Charting Your Route to Party Island" for these strategies.

But keep in mind what Annie has done: She's started with a very small sum of money in her retirement plan, leveraged it, and has developed sizable assets in her R01K. She has mastered the art of combining real estate, leverage, and the current tax code to a fantastic advantage for herself. She knows that making safe and secure investments locally, with maximum control and reasonable returns, she will "retire", that is, she will begin receiving TAX FREE income at an early age. She will obtain property for her own use through her retirement plan using PIK distributions, and she will have a considerable retirement beyond any amount the boys on Wall Street can promise her.

To summarize, you don't need a lot of money to seed your R01K. You need a small amount that you can leverage or even co-invest with your T01K. Once the Solo 401K has been established, you have the ability to contribute to your R01K. Even if that contribution is small, you can make it grow until it's your main retirement vehicle. This is the best party ever.

Points to Remember

1. Only Roth 401K money may be rolled over to your R01K.
2. Roth IRAs may not be transferred.
3. Contributions to the R01K need not be large.
4. Leverage and "piggy backing" on other investments makes your R01K grow.
5. You can distribute property from your R01K tax and penalty free after age 59 ½.
6. Your R01K works in conjunction with your Roth IRA to distribute tax-free income before age 59 ½.
7. Use your R01K and Roth IRA to establish a 72t distribution.
8. Your Roth IRA protects your R01K from RMDs during retirement.
9. Your R01K gets all the same advantages of your Traditional 401K, plus a great deal more.
10. Using your R01K, you pay no UBIT, no Short Term Capital Gains, No Long Term Capital Gains, you avoid 1031 Exchanges and Depreciation Recapture, and you pay NO Income Tax, ever.

12. Party with Yourself

By now you should have two great parties going on. You've got the great party going on in your T01K, and you've started to party on Party Island in your R01K. The beauty of this arrangement is that the T01K can party together with the R01K. This is a great benefit to most people, since the majority of the money available to them will reside in their T01K. Let's go back to Annie to see how she uses this to her advantage.

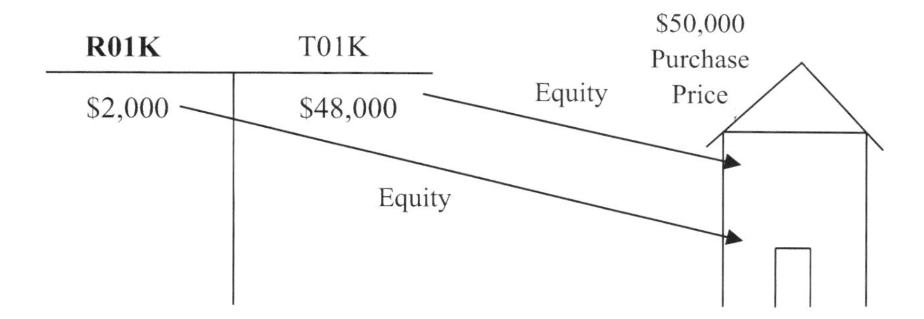

Purchase

Annie buys a fix'r upper to do a fix-n-flip for $50,000. She invests $48,000 from her T01K and co-invests $2,000 from her R01K. The $50,000 represents her acquisition costs plus her improvements. The house ultimately sells for $75,000. Annie splits the profit according to the same proportion as the investment. Her R01K gets $1,000 and her T01K gets $24,000.

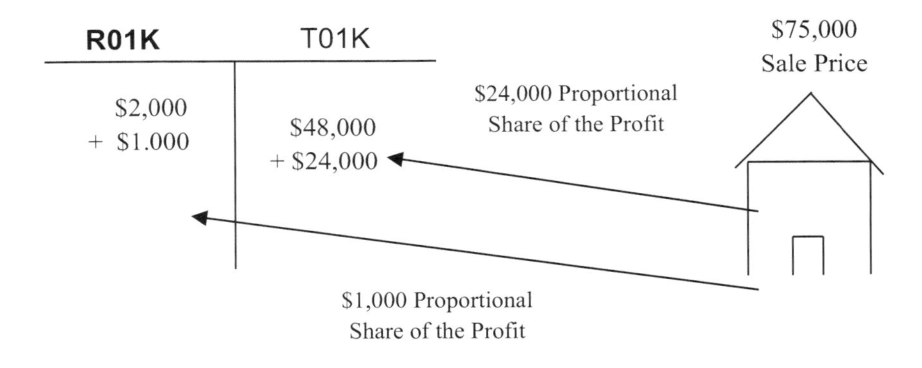

Sale

Please note, and I can't stress this enough, the return of the investment is ABSOLUTELY proportionate to the amounts invested from each account. That's the difference between "co-investing" and "commingling." You may not, under any circumstances, bleed funds from the T01K to the R01K.

Now I know some of you are thinking "Hey, leverage is such a great thing. Why doesn't Annie's R01K borrow money from her own T01K, just like she did with her dad? She could borrow the majority of the money from her T01K, pay it 10%, then keep all the profit in her R01K. That would work, wouldn't it?"

If that were to happen, Annie's transaction would look like this:

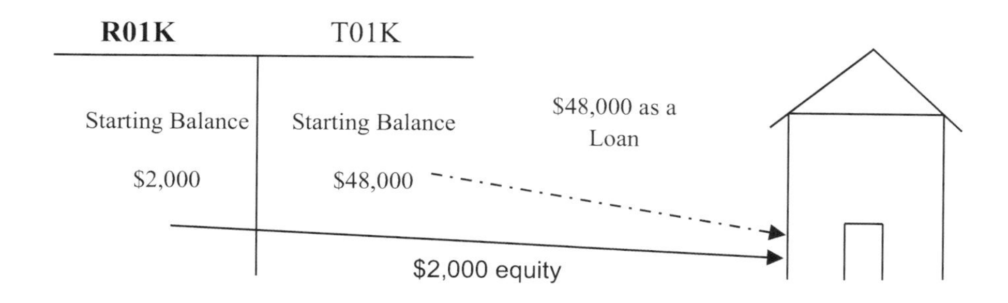

Purchase

Notice that the T01K is acting as a lender, not as an equity partner.

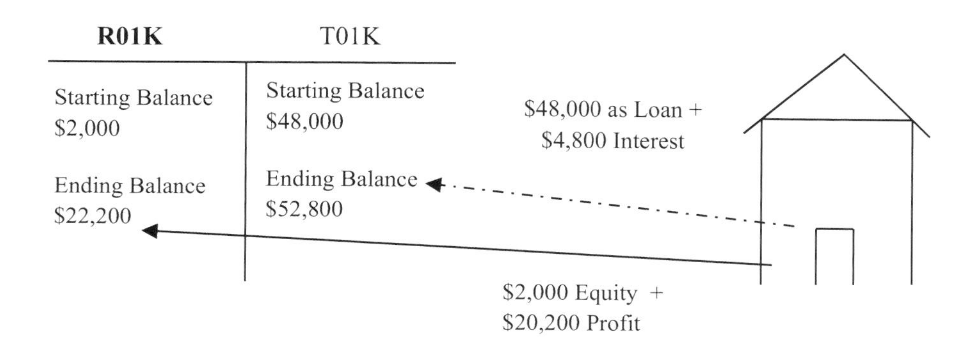

Sale

This seems like a great idea, and, after all, it's exactly what Annie did with her dad, right? Although I know of no law, prohibition or regulation against this, I can tell you: DON'T DO IT!

Take a moment to put yourself into the position of an IRS auditor. You know that first and foremost highly taxable money must pay its tax, right? And you know that a conversion from a traditional plan to a Roth is a highly taxable transaction, right? And you know that people will do anything to avoid paying taxes, right? So here we have a situation where the same person's Roth invested with their own traditional plan. They should split the profit proportionately, yet the Roth came out ahead the big winner. Is this a legitimate transaction, or is it just using some accounting dodge to circumvent the requirements for conversion? Well, let's see who can tell the IRS agent who can judge this? Hey! It's the IRS agent.

This is one of those cases where something may be allowed in the regulations, but it is a horribly bad idea. You do not want to be audited. You do not want to be fined. You do not want your plan dissolved. Remember, the IRS can judge your actions based on intent. Is this "leveraged" transaction legitimate, or was its intent to avoid paying tax. Let your friendly IRS agent be the judge of that, because he certainly will be. Is there any doubt in your mind as to the outcome?

Annie, the smart investor, knows to steer clear of trouble spots like this. She can take her relatively small R01K and piggy back on larger deals as long as she does it correctly. She also knows she can use leverage to grow her R01K if she does it correctly as well. She just wants to steer clear of any transaction that has the whiff of impropriety.

Annie also knows that without the whiff of impropriety, fantastic things can be done in her R01K. Annie has co-invested with enough people that she has earned their trust. People know if they get on board with her, that she will have done her homework, assessed the risks, developed at least two exit strategies and will have determined a reasonable profit for everyone involved. That means she has people who are willing to lend money to her on low risk investments. (Need I point out to you that every investment has risk, regardless of the work that you do to reduce it?)

Even knowing that, Annie has developed a cadre of people willing to consider the investment opportunities Annie brings to them. Annie's R01K can buy a house for $90,500. It's a three bedroom – one bath home, but to make it more desirable it needs another bath. Annie can add that bath and have some minor touch-up done for $2,500. She borrows $93,000 from her willing investors at 10%, due in three months. After installing a renter at $1,300 per month, Annie has the property reappraised. It's now worth $155,000. Taking a loan at 70% loan-to-value, Annie gets $108,500 which allows her to pay her lenders $102,300. Annie's R01K now owns a $155,000 house with $6,200 in cash. The only part of the entire transaction the R01K performed was paying some transfer fees to retitle the property.

So if you've followed that narrative, you might be asking yourself "Wait! Annie can take her R01K from $2,000 to $155,000 in three months?" The answer is "YES! Yes, she can." You then might ask "Well then, why doesn't she take it from ZERO to $155,000?" Remember we talked about a "whiff of impropriety"? If Annie had $0 in her R01K, then performed the above transaction, the IRS would look at it and say "Annie, you have just made a $155,000 contribution to your R01K, and that's illegal." But you see, Annie started with $2,000 in her R01K and part of that original contribution participated in the transaction. She could have started with $500 or $50 as long as the money she contributed to her plan participated in the acquisition of the property.

Let's take a look. Annie's self directing her Solo R01K, so imagine that she deposits $50 into it. She buys some penny stock in a bio-med company. They cure the common cold, and now her stock is worth

$5,000,000. Is there any impropriety there? No, of course not. Just as with the $93,000 house, her small investment garnered a great return.

Now as I said, getting to party on Party Island is a little more difficult than any of the other parties. Annie has built up a body of knowledge and experience that allowed her to gain the trust of people willing to lend to her. In the example above, Annie's greatest asset was her good name and the trust she'd earned from others. This didn't happen on her first transaction in the real estate game. Annie did what any good investor would do: she found a mentor, she participated in some other people's low risk transactions, "piggy-backing" on them. She moved on to do some of her own small scale investments, then did some small scale investments with some other people piggy-backing on hers. When the people riding piggy-back earned great returns, they then became willing to lend more to her. In the real life transaction that the example is based on, the investor who did this for his co-investors had already owned three rental properties in his own name and had been a landlord for a number of years.

Annie has leveraged her greatest asset into an asset worth $155,000 plus $6,200 after the refinancing of the house and paying off her lenders. That asset wasn't her $2,000 in her R01K That asset was her good name.

Just as in any endeavor, making any strategy work for you is a matter of treating people fairly and well. If you thought this book was about making scads of money, then you have to understand that you have to make scads of friends and satisfied clients. The first chapter of this book closed by saying that you have to bring friends. Playing the real estate game is not Solitaire, and it's not Rugby. If done correctly, when the game is over, you've won, your co-investors have won, the buyer has won, the renter has won, and the community has won.

Now that's a party!

13. Party with a Purpose

We've addressed saving oodles of money on taxes. We've avoided Unrelated Business Income Tax, Long Term Capital Gains, Short Term Capital Gains and Income Tax. Money that would have gone to the government now can stay in our families' coffers. That should be comforting to you in no small measure. But our taxes, at least to some degree, go to support things like infrastructure and safety in our communities. If you're going to live tax free, I strongly suggest you consider some options that benefit the community. I'm not talking about giving to charity, although I encourage it. Rather I'm talking about investments that benefit you financially as well as making your community, or rather, any community a better place to live.

Consider Milwaukee. Milwaukee, like many communities, has suffered white-flight. An industrial city, much of the employment base has downsized, moved, or is now out of business. Like most of the rest of the country, the housing market has been decimated by the lending practices that led up to the crash of 2008. On the bright side, Milwaukee's unemployment has stabilized, and the city has instituted programs to help people get into homes they can legitimately afford. The problem with this is the people who can legitimately afford a nice house don't qualify under the more stringent lending requirements now imposed by the banking system after their unqualified lending fiasco.

For example, there are hundreds of houses available in the $30,000 to $60,000 range. Much of the population could afford that house according to their income. Even if a person bought a house for $60,000 and financed all of it, the principle and interest payments would come to $292.12 with an APR of 4.163% for a 30 year note. Even with a 10 year note the monthly mortgage payments would be $612.13. Yet most people wouldn't qualify for the loan simply because there are no programs for 100% financing offered by most banks. Even with 95% financing a person would need $3,000 for a down payment. Yet many people have employment that would support payments up to $700 to $900 per month.

What does this mean to you, the investor?

Let's look at a real life situation.

Some people I know bought a two-bedroom, one-bath house in Milwaukee for $16,000, fully furnished. A 93 year old woman passed away, and her 73 year old daughter did not want to mess with the house. It had couches, lamps, tables, chairs, beds, appliances, a fully equipped work bench and an unattached garage. The house needed some work. The toilet had leaked causing the floor some damage. There was some rotten wood around the door of the garage and a little add-on mud room had shifted, pulling away from the house. Paint and repairs amounted to $1,500 dollars.

So with $17,500 in the project, the house rented for $750 per month which was standard for the area for two-bed, one-bath homes. This resulted in a 29.22% cash-on-cash return for these investors. However, they had invested to help the neighborhood and the community. Absentee landlords, no matter how kind hearted, do not help the community as much as home ownership.

Since the neighborhood and most of the clientele that would live there would fall into the category of people not qualifying for conventional financing, the investors structured a rent-to-own deal for a qualified individual. To show that the renter was actually building equity in the house, a premium had to be charged to the rent. This is a requirement by banks to show the amount of equity the renter has acquired over the term of the contract, so that when the renter applies for conventional financing, the total of the premiums paid reflect the equity built.

The investors set up a rental agreement with their occupant for $900 per month. The premium for the equity in the rent to own contract was $150, which over 12 months amounted to $1,800. The rent-to-own contract set the rental term to five years, with a balloon at the end of that term. The renter was expected to acquire conventional financing somewhere in that time. The sale price of the house was set at $35,000. This allowed the renter to build equity and to establish good credit during the five year period. The renter would have 20% equity in 3 years and 10 months, but may qualify for a 10% or 15% equity loan depending on his situation. Of course, if the five year term were reached without refinancing, the contract could be renegotiated, or a new renter could be found.

This was great for the renter, but the investor's cash-on-cash return jumped from 29.22% to 38.77%. This return includes paying all the property taxes, reserves for vacancies and maintenance, as well as a property management fee of 10%. (Remember, you're here to party, not jiggle toilet handles in the middle of the night.)

The long and short of this is that investors can earn handsome returns while improving the quality of the neighborhoods and providing home ownership to people that might not qualify through normal channels. This truly is a win-win-win situation.

Other ways to benefit the community exist as well. Many large homes were built in the run-away 2000's and now sit idle. Repurposing these structures has advantages similar to those found in providing homes to individuals. Any councilman, alderman, mayor or city planner will tell you that vacant structures, regardless of their size or beauty, detract from their community. These large houses can be converted to office space, business incubators, youth centers, or any need the community might identify. Check with your local officials to discover what they might have in mind for these structures. Like much unwanted real estate today, these large houses are selling for pennies on the dollar.

If you are creative, you can make wonderful returns while at the same time benefiting deserving individuals and their communities.

14. Never Leave Party Island

At some point you'll have to consider retirement. I don't mean retirement as laid out in this book. Our concept of retirement is doing what you want, when you want, with whom you want, and not having to worry about your money. If you're a neurologist, keep on working with patients, as long as you love your work. If you're a Wall Street whiz, and you've made your million before thirty, then go open a restaurant that features your grandmother's favorite recipes (an actual case). Retirement doesn't mean you quit working, it just means you don't HAVE to work any more. But in the classic sense, the sense based on age, you'll have to consider retiring. That age has been determined for you by the IRS. That age is 70.

Now let's assume you've done most things right. You've started your Sol01K which includes your T01K and your R01K. You've used the advantages of the Sol01K to full advantage. You've rolled your traditional IRAs, your old 401Ks, your 403Bs, your SIMPLEs, SEPs, SARSEPs and Keoughs to your personal plan. You've seeded the R01K either with rollovers from R01Ks from other companies, or you've contributed a small amount of your ordinary income that you've generated in your small business. You've co-invested in something that makes good returns or even great returns and now you have a sizable sum in your Sol01K. If you've planned and executed correctly, you should have most of your money in the Roth R01K side, and an equally sizable amount in the Traditional side. You've opened a little Roth IRA that's just sitting and waiting for its day to come. You turn 70 and now it's time for your little Roth IRA to shine. Let's review why we wanted an R01K instead of a Roth IRA.

The R01K outshines the Roth IRA because:

- R01Ks have no Unrelated Debt Financed Income (UDFI)
- R01Ks have limited Unrelated Business Income Tax (UBIT)
- R01Ks allow Participant Loans, not available in Roth IRAs
- R01Ks have no Income Limits
- R01Ks have no Custodians (you are your own trustee)

For those of you who play chess, this will make complete sense. The most powerful piece on the board is the queen. The least powerful are the little pawns. But if a pawn advances to the eighth row, a magical thing happens to our little friend: it can become any piece on the board, even a queen! Yes, the weakest piece on the board becomes filled with power, and so too the Roth IRA becomes our ticket to stay on Party Island forever, including our children, our grandchildren and generations to follow.

For you see, as powerful as the R01K is, it has a horrible weakness. That weakness is called RMD. RMD stands for Required Minimum Distribution. Designed to distribute traditional IRAs and 401Ks over a person's life expectancy, the RMD was the attempt by the IRS to empty the retirement plan before a participant died. The original life expectancy table for traditional plans maxed out at age 100, but with greater life expectancy, the tables now run to 115. Regardless of how long the tables project, the net effect is that the IRS forces you to take distributions according to their schedule whether you want that money or not. In the case of traditional plans, the RMDs assure that money will flow out in a highly taxable stream into the waiting coffers of Uncle Sam. Even though not taxable the RMDs apply to the R01K as well. The Roth provisions are, after all, instituted under the original 401K structure, so the 401K rules must be followed.

I can hear many of you right now, wondering why it would make any difference to the recipients if they were forced to take tax free money. If the money's tax free, who cares? A person with $1M in their 401K before RMD will still have $1M after RMD, right?

That is very true, if you only look at the day the person took their RMD. But let's take a look at the affect of time plus tax. Remember that in a tax free environment money grows completely uninhibited: basically it's a wild party! Once placed into a taxable environment, growth is much more restricted: a tea party. Here's what happens.

We'll take a person who has $1,000,000 in his R01K at age 70, then withdraws it all. It's tax free, so there is no impact of taxes on his withdrawal. When he withdraws it from his Roth, he places it in exactly the same investment which resided in his Roth before the distribution. However as he ages, he must pay tax on his earnings, so the growth is restricted. We'll compare that to tax free growth as if he had left it in a tax free environment. Our fellow is earning 6% and is in a 25% income tax bracket for people married filing jointly (based on 2010 tax brackets).

Age	Ex-401K Amt	6%	Tax	After Tax Return		Tax Free Environment
Start of 70	$1,000,000	$60,000	$15,000	$45,000		$1,000,000
End of 70	$1,045,000	$62,700	$15,675	$47,025		$1,060,000
End of 71	$1,092,025	$65,522	$16,380	$49,141		$1,123,600
End of 72	$1,141,166	$68,470	$17,117	$51,352		$1,191,016
End of 73	$1,192,519	$71,551	$17,888	$53,663		$1,262,477
End of 74	$1,246,182	$74,771	$18,693	$56,078		$1,338,226
End of 75	$1,302,260	$78,136	$19,534	$58,602		$1,418,519
End of 76	$1,360,862	$81,652	$20,413	$61,239		$1,503,630
End of 77	$1,422,101	$85,326	$21,332	$63,995		$1593,848
End of 78	$1,486,095	$89,166	$22,291	$66,874		$1,689,479
End of 79	$1,552,969	$93,178	$23,295	$69,884		$1,790,848
Start of 80	**$1,622,853**					**$1,898,299**

Observe that at age 70 our gentleman has $1,000,000 earning 6%, i.e. $60,000. Since he is in the 25% tax bracket, $15,000 disappears in the form of taxes, leaving him with an after-tax return of $45,000. Year by year then, you can see the effect of taxes on his savings. The last column shows the same growth in a tax free environment, whether an R01K or a Roth IRA. His 6% return amounts to over $275,000 that he could have earned if he had not had a tax burden. Think of it this way, he lost over a quarter of a million in 10 years. And that's only a 6% return.

Ok, let's digest that for a minute. Our guy takes a completely tax free distribution, keeps it in exactly the same investment he's been in all along, earns the same return he's been earning, and winds up a quarter of a million poorer in ten years.

Oh, but why would he take all of it at once? What if he stuck to the IRS schedule and just took a little at a time, according to the RMD? He wouldn't lose all his tax free status on day one, then, would he? Let's take a look. (Watch out: For the math impared, this gets really tricky.) Let's start by describing what will happen. Our guy has a million in his R01K at age 70. He has to divide the balance of his account by a number given him in the IRS tables. That number happens to be 27.4. When he does that, that gives him an amount he MUST withdraw that year or face a 50% penalty.

On a million dollars, that's $36,496 he must move out of his R01K into a taxable account. As before, he moves the RMD into exactly the same investment that it was in before the move. In our example, he moves the RMD at the beginning of the year (for you picky types that like to know all the assumptions). After the distribution, his R01K account earns 6%. Since his distribution is in the same investment, it also earns 6%, but he must pay tax on it. Being in a 25% tax bracket, his net after-tax return on his taxable account works out to 4.5%.

The following table shows the net effect of taxes on distributions based on a $1,000,000 R01K at the start of the year, taking RMD for a person aged 70, then earning 6% in both non-taxable and taxable accounts in a 25% tax bracket when married filing jointly.

If you take the Roth amount ($1,154,429.50), add the After Tax Account ($653,622.10) which is all the RMDs plus interest earned – less taxes, and the Interest Earned Net Tax ($29,412.99) which is the amount earned in the taxable account in his 80th year, you get $1,837,464.60, which is $60,833.96 less than if the entire amount had been able to grow tax free in the Roth. $60,000 is lost to taxes and the interest that should have been earned on that tax.

If you lose $60,000 in ten years, how much do your children or grandchildren lose in their life times?

So you can see that passing on the Roth, uninterrupted by taxes, is a huge benefit to someone's family. That's why our gal, Annie Investor, has opened her Roth IRA in a very small amount some time in the distant past. Not only was she able to use her Roth IRA to develop tax free income before age 59 ½, she now uses it to eliminate RMD! She knows that the Roth IRA has NO RMD!

Annie can take the money she wants, as she sees fit, then can pass on the rest to her heirs who also can allow it to grow over their lifetimes.

	Balance Start of Age 70 $1,000,000.00	RMD Factor	RMD	After Tax Account	Interest Earned	Tax	Interest Earned Net Tax
70	$1,021,313.87	27.4	$36,496.35	$36,496.35	$2,189.78	$547.45	$1,642.34
71	$1,041,740.15	26.5	$38,540.15	$76,678.83	$4,600.73	$1,150.18	$3,450.55
72	$1,061,110.00	25.6	$40,692.97	$120,822.35	$7,249.34	$1,812.34	$5,437.01
73	$1,079,239.09	24.7	$42,959.92	$169,219.28	$10,153.16	$2,538.29	$7,614.87
74	$1,095,926.48	23.8	$45,346.18	$222,180.33	$13,330.82	$3,332.70	$9,998.11
75	$1,110,953.60	22.9	$47,857.05	$280,035.49	$16,802.13	$4,200.53	$12,601.60
76	$1,124,083.05	22.0	$50,497.89	$343,134.98	$20,588.10	$5,147.02	$15,441.07
77	$1,135,323.88	21.2	$53,022.79	$411,598.84	$24,695.93	$6,173.98	$18,521.95
78	$1,144,160.39	20.3	$55,927.28	$486,048.07	$29,162.88	$7,290.72	$21,872.16
79	$1,150,614.63	19.5	$58,674.89	$566,595.13	$33,995.71	$8,498.93	$25,496.78
80	**$1,154,429.50**	18.7	$61,530.19	**$653,622.10**	$39,217.33	$9,804.33	**$29,412.99**

If Annie's grand-daughter is 40 when she inherits $100,000 from Annie's Roth IRA, she will have to begin taking withdrawals since it's an inherited Roth. If she continues to invest and grow her inherited Roth, she could reasonably retire with $475,000 in Grandma Annie's Roth, and she would have withdrawn over $230,000 tax free in 25 years. Her children can inherit this also. Annie's lineage could be given tax free incomes for their entire lives. Your family, your children, your grandchildren, all your heirs could live on party island forever.

15. You MUST Party

You must party. You have no choice. I'm serious. Living on Party Island is not an option. It is an absolute necessity. You have two enemies that are lurking to suck the life out of you, out of your savings, your investments, your retirement and most of all, your peace of mind.

Did you ever wonder why people are moved to celebrate? Even the most restrictive societies have some holidays, holy days, or feast days that allow adherents to kick up their heals. As the old saying goes "All work and no play make Jack a dull boy."

But Party Island is not just a vacation spot to chill and relax. It is the refuge and sanctuary from your two worst enemies. These enemies don't lay in wait for you in a dark alley. They don't break into your house in the middle of the night. They don't beat you over the head and grab your wallet. They do work in conjunction to take everything you've worked for, and they conspire to lead you to believe they don't work against you. These two sneaky thieves are named Inflation and Taxes. Furthermore, there are interests that use these guys to their advantage. They employ them to make your decision making process difficult, and to make your deciding upon the right choice almost impossible.

Let's talk about the more insidious thief: Inflation. Inflation erodes the value of your money day by day and week by week. Inflation is particularly crafty and cunning. It lulls you into thinking you're okay, but it really steals you blind while gulling you into a false sense of security. Imagine a man buys his true love a fine Tiffany necklace. It has large diamonds inset in white, green and rose gold. She wears it only on rare occasions otherwise keeping it in their safe. Some years later she desires to have it appraised only to find out that the gold setting is original, but all the stones are now Zircon, practically worthless. The necklace never left her possession, and only she and her husband had the combination to the safe.

A more real life example: I went through some old clothes in my attic. I found a top coat I had worn in 1972 when I graduated from high school. In one of the pockets I found a coupon for 33 gallons of gas. I was thrilled. I took the coupon to the gas station, but the attendant said that, although they'd honor the coupon, he would only give me 2 ½ gallons for it. The coupon was a $10 bill, and when I graduated from high school gas was 30 cents a gallon. At $4.00 per gallon, my $10 bill was not worth as much.

Inflation is insidious. Like a shadow at night, it's hard to define. The figures that our government gives us today about the amount of inflation are considerably different than the ones they gave us in 1970 – 1980. That is, the way they figure inflation is considerably different. If you were to use the same criteria for inflation that they did 30 years ago, you might find that inflation has been running between 7% - 8% for the last decade, rather than the 3 – 4% that's being reported. What does that mean to you?

Have you ever heard the expression "the magic of compound interest?" Inflation is the black magic practitioner, and he practices "the magic of confound interest." If inflation has been running 7% per year, your money shrinks at that rate. The $100,000 you have in your retirement right now will be worth only $93,000 by the end of this year. Oh, don't get me wrong. Your statement may read considerably higher than that, but the original $100,000 will have dwindled to $93,000 in purchasing power. Oh, and every dollar you earn will have shrunk to 93 cents as well. So this is what it will look like in the real world.

Let's say you have $100,000 in a reasonably sound investment that pays pretty well, about 7.526% at year's end. You've earned $7,526.00 on your $100,000 giving you a total of $107,526. Pretty simple, right? Now sneaky old inflation comes along, and he's been shrinking those dollars day by day. So your number in your account is 107526, but when you multiply 107526 by .07, you get $100,000! Your real purchasing power went down by $7,526 which means your $107,526 account can now only buy $100,000 worth of stuff. Pretty simple or pretty scary? The first year it's simple, over time, it's scary. Remember the magic of "confound interest?" It's where scary begins to grow. After 10 years of getting 7.526% returns, your account now reads $206,619. Hey! You've doubled your money in 10 years!! That's great, and that should give you a warm fuzzy. And when you figure what our friendly thief inflation has done for you, a warm fuzzy is about all you'll have left. You're right! That $206,619 has the same purchasing power it had 10 years earlier when the number was only $100,000. If you've ever read Alice in Wonderland, there's a chapter where the Red Queen makes Alice run and run. After running till she drops, Alice finds she's under the same tree they've always been under. She remarks to the queen:

> `Well, in *our* country,' said Alice, still panting a little, `you'd generally get to somewhere else -- if you ran very fast for a long time, as we've been doing.'

`A slow sort of country!' said the Queen. `Now, *here*, you see, it takes all the running *you* can do, to keep in the same place. If you want to get somewhere else, you must run at least twice as fast as that!'

The author, Lewis Carroll, was in reality a mathematician named Charles Dodson. Could this passage reveal something he knew of inflation? Whether he wrote of inflation or not, he definitely did not write about Inflation and his henchman, Taxes. Together they pick your pocket, take your cash, put back the wallet, and you barely know it's been pilfered. Look at the example above again.

It's obvious that to keep up with 7% inflation we need 7.526% just to break even. But we haven't figured in taxes. You see, the IRS doesn't care about inflation. There's no deduction or credit for the amount your money is shrinking. You pay the tax on the number of dollars you earn, not on the value of the dollars you earn. (Prepare to be really scared.)

In our example above, you've set aside $100,000, and you've earned 7.526%. Depending if that return was interest, dividend or capital gains, you could pay anywhere from 10 – 33.5%. Just to make things easy, let's say that was all dividend and interest income taxable at 25%. So although you earned $7,526 on your $100,000, Uncle IRS will take a quarter of that in taxes, leaving you with $5,644.50 to add to your account. You now have $105,644.50 which is shrinking by 7%. At the end of the year, you've lost $7,395.12 in purchasing power. So the real value of your $105,644.50 is really $98,249.39. You had to earn $7,526 to wind up $1,751 in the hole.

Next year your $105,644.50 will earn $7,951.76 of which you'll give $1,987.92 to Uncle IRS leaving you with an account balance of $111,607.60, BUT your true purchasing power will have fallen to

$96,529.42. Yes, you've earned over $15,000 to end up $3,571 poorer than when you started. Do you see how underhanded and insidious these two bandits are? Want to know what this looks like in 10 years? At 7.526% return in a 25% tax bracket the number on your account will say you have 173,168.5 slips of green paper to your name, but the purchasing power of that paper will be $83,000. If you want to keep up to inflation and taxes (keep up, not get ahead), you need to consistently earn 10.04% on your investments. TO BREAK EVEN!

You may be saying "Yeah, at 7%, that's what you need, but inflation has been a lot lower than that." Please go to the website *www.shadowstats.com* for more information on a truer picture of inflation. It's been higher than has been reported.

Now although inflation is our big thief, you can't even begin to arm yourself against him unless you've eliminated his toady, Taxes. Consider the following:

If inflation is running at 7%, you need to earn at least the following returns just to break even.

7% Inflation						
Tax Bracket	10%	15%	25%	28%	33%	35%
Break Even Return	8.36%	8.86%	10.04%	10.45%	11.23%	11.58%

Compare that to what you need to break even in a tax free environment:

7% Inflation in Tax Free Environment (R01K)						
Tax Bracket	10%	15%	25%	28%	33%	35%
Break Even Return	7.526%	7.526%	7.526%	7.526%	7.526%	7.526%

Which return is more reasonable? Which return is easier to exceed? Which return is more available? Can you see why it's critical to work in a tax free environment?

With the following chart you can pick your necessary rate of return for the break-even point on inflation.

		Tax Bracket (Married Filing Jointly)					
		10%	15%	25%	28%	33%	35%
Rate of Inflation	1%	1.12%	1.19%	1.35%	1.40%	1.51%	1.55%
	2%	2.27%	2.40%	2.72%	2.83%	3.05%	3.14%
	3%	3.44%	3.64%	4.12%	4.30%	4.62%	4.76%
	4%	4.63%	4.90%	5.56%	5.79%	6.22%	6.41%
	5%	5.85%	6.19%	7.02%	7.31%	7.86%	8.10%
	6%	7.09%	7.51%	8.51%	8.87%	9.53%	9.82%
	7%	8.36%	8.86%	10.04%	10.45%	11.23%	11.58%
	8%	9.66%	10.23%	11.59%	12.08%	12.98%	13.38%
	9%	10.99%	11.64%	13.19%	13.74%	14.76%	15.22%
	10%	12.35%	13.07%	14.81%	15.43%	16.58%	17.09%

You should see now how inflation and taxes double-team your earnings to rob you of everything you've saved for. You should also see by now that working in the Roth environment is the first step to breaking up this nefarious team. You will be able to address inflation only if you eliminate taxes. I know I started by saying that we should learn to love the tax code, and I still mean it. Love the tax code: hate taxes!

It's time to party, we have to party like our financial futures depend on it.

Points to Remember

1. Inflation is the sneakiest thief of wealth in the United States.
2. Inflation has not been accurately reported since the mid-1980s.
3. The decrease in value of money due to inflation is greater than earnings of the same percentage.
4. Understanding how inflation works is critical to beating inflation.
5. It's difficult to beat inflation without first beating taxes.
6. Inflation and taxes give a one-two punch to your finances.
7. The R01K allows you to eliminate taxes.
8. By eliminating taxes you allow yourself safer investments.
9. More modest returns become profitable in a R01K.
10. It is absolutely necessary to invest within an R01K.

16. Party 'til You're Golden!

Since I started the first chapter with a tirade about the gold standard, I feel I must apologize to all the gold bugs reading this book. Many of you who are not gold bugs may have thought to yourselves "Well, my advisor tells me to own some precious metal. It can't be all bad." Let me point out that gold as an investment is nothing like the gold standard. We have a fiat currency system that is immutable. But gold, as an investment, is excellent. Not only can gold certificates be held in 401Ks, but the actual metal itself can constitute part of your portfolio.

As you remember, collectibles may not be held in any retirement plan, but certain coins minted to a standard set by the IRS may be held in secured depositories. The gold that's allowed in retirement plans must meet a standard of purity, called fine. Gold must be .995 fine or 99.5% gold. It is the requirement for fine that prohibits the inclusion of circulated coins from retirement plans, not the fact that they're collectible. When gold coins were in common usage, because of the softness of gold, a base metal had to be added to keep the coins from wearing out rapidly. Consequently these coins don't have the purity necessary to qualify for retirement plans. It's possible that the degree of fine was established to exclude circulated coins.

Here is a list of coins, ingots, bars and rounds that may be held in a retirement plan:

Gold

- American Eagle coins
- U.S. Buffalo Bullion coins
- Canadian Maple Leaf coins
- Mexican Gold Libertads
- Austrian Philharmonic coins
- Australian Kangaroos
- Australian Gold Nugget coins
- Chinese Gold Panda
- Credit Suisse – PAMP Suisse Bars
- Various bars and rounds .995 fine

Silver

- American Eagle coins
- Canadian Maple Leaf coins
- Austrian Vienna Philharmonic coins
- Australian Kookaburra coins
- Chinese Silver Panda
- Mexican Silver Libertad
- Chinese Silver Panda
- Various bars and rounds .999

Platinum

- American Eagle coins
- Canadian Maple Leaf coins
- Austrian Philharmonic coins
- Australian Koala coins
- Various bars and rounds .9995

Palladium

- Canadian Maple Leaf coins
- Russian 25 Roubles
- Various bars and rounds .9995

Also, any bar or ingot made with a NYMEX- or COMEX- approved refiner/assayer hallmark may be added to an R01K. Please note: It doesn't matter what the country of origin is, the only criteria is the level of fine that the coin or bar might contain. Be cautious! There is much misinformation found on the net and the list above could change at any time if another country were to produce coins meeting IRS specifications.

Many people are interested in gold and precious metals, but the inclusion of them in your 401K must be seriously considered before embarking on it. Remember that any metal, regardless of its form, must be held in a secured depository. Deciding on the correct depository can entail as much research as buying the metal itself. Some questions to consider:

- Where is the depository located?
- Is the proximity of the depository important to you?
- Is the depository also a trader or dealer in gold?
- If they trade or deal, will they have conflicting interests?
- Do they inventory everything to you or do they use the LIFO method of inventory?
- How secure is the depository?
- How is your metal insured?
- What is the cost to store and inventory your metal?

These are but a few questions that one must consider when storing precious metals, much less buying them.

Other commodities may offer as good of a hedge or better against inflation or the devaluation of the dollar. Oil offers a good alternative to precious metals in this regard. Since oil is being consumed at an ever increasing rate, its price will ultimately go up. The volatility of it may scare off the more conservative investors, but its worth investigating as an alternative if you're considering gold as a hedge against the devaluation of the dollar.

Another factor in holding precious metals is the fact that it's a non-income producing asset. If you are of a certain age, the term "gold brick" or "gold bricking" is an apt term for this investment. A "gold bricker" was an employee who did nothing while on the job and your metal acts the same way. While you're waiting for the crash in the economy or while you're waiting for the soaring rise in the price of the metal to come, your metal sits idly by, happily costing you storage fees.

Although some investment in the metal itself may be wise, a great alternative would be to buy some mining or oil drilling stocks. Not only would you receive the boost of the rise in the price of the commodity when it comes, but your mining stock would produce income while you wait. You could invest in mining, exploration or refining to get the income from a front line investment. Of course if you invest in a company that has a mine collapse, or an oil company that becomes the next BP, you could suffer a setback.

To hedge against disasters that could befall front line investments, you might want to consider "Pick and Shovel" investments. The term "pick and shovel" comes from the gold rush of 1849. Literally millions of people in the nascent country of the United States crossed the frontier to find their fortunes when someone shouted "Gold!" at Sutter's Mill, California. Hundreds of thousands migrated from all over the world, and a few of them did find great fortunes. Some found small fortunes. Many found some gold, and most found little. The true profits from the rush were made by the merchants. The general stores selling picks and shovels made money whether the miners themselves did or not.

Modern "pick and shovel" investing consists of buying stock in companies that provide goods and services to the front line companies. The firms making diamond drills and such will thrive even if the mining and oil companies decline. One firm that has been making equipment for the oil industry now provides its products to the energy sector drilling for geothermal purposes.

To capitalize on the precious metal craze, a blend of metals, mining and oil company stock, including pick and shovel investing should provide the hedge against inflation or a falling dollar while providing the savvy investor with the income and security provided by each level.

You wouldn't drink and drive would you? You'd appoint a designated driver for your night out on the town, wouldn't you? Then you would want to party in your retirement plan as safely and wisely as well. Use a variety of "precious metal" investments to provide the safety and income you need.

Points to Remember

1. Gold and other precious metals may be held in your R01K.
2. Coins are limited by their degree of fine, that is, their level of purity.
3. Country of origin doesn't matter for coins, only their content.
4. Precious metals may be a hedge against inflation or a falling dollar, but they produce no income.
5. Oil may be a good alternative to precious metal.
6. "Front line" investments offer income as well as the opportunity to benefit from the price of the commodity.
7. Front line companies may incur risks due to disasters.
8. "Pick and shovel" companies avoid the risk of front line companies.
9. Pick and shovel companies provide goods and services to other industries as well.
10. A blend of commodities, front line companies and pick and shovel investments provide the best mix to allow you to hedge against inflation, provide income and give your portfolio safety.

17. Party the World Over!

Just to follow up on the last chapter, I want to point out that you can own land anywhere in the world in your 401K. Like the T-shirt says from the Solomon Islands, "Ho hum. Just another crummy day in paradise." If you want to own land in the Solomons, you may do so. Caiman Islands? Yep. Belize? Sure. Just about anywhere in the world is fine to own land.

What countries don't qualify? As of the writing of this book, the following countries are considered restricted. These countries are restricted for a variety of reasons, and they could change as rapidly as the revolution in Egypt happened in mid 2011. As governments change and allegiances shift, this list will alter accordingly.

- Armenia
- Kazakhstan
- Syria
- Azerbaijan
- North Korea
- Tajikistan
- Albania
- Kyrgyzstan
- Turkmenistan
- Belarus
- Laos
- Ukraine
- Cambodia
- Libya
- Uzbekistan
- Macau
- Vietnam
- Cuba
- Moldova
- Georgia

- Mongolia
- Iraq
- Iran
- Sudan

Besides being able to buy land in non-restricted countries, your 401K can establish trading accounts in these nations as well. In the previous chapter we addressed gold and precious metals as a hedge against inflation, or more importantly, against the prospect of a rapidly falling dollar. If you are very concerned with a dollar crisis, you can do a portion, or even all of your investing in countries that may be protected against this. Think about it. Even if you buy gold as a hedge, and the dollar crashes, what are you going to get with your gold? If you hold mining stocks denominated in US currency, what happens to your great stock when the dollar heads south?

With a little homework and some research on the net, you should be able to find four or five nations that have stable governments, are net exporters, and have little or no national debt. If you are comfortable investing elsewhere, then keep in mind your 401K can invest wherever you like. When the US currency falls, it would be great to have some currencies that are more stable during that period. Keep in mind that your R01K can invest anywhere you see fit. Party the world over.

18. The Party's not Over, It's Just Started!

Well, fellow partiers, this book is done. You should have learned the following:

1. As good as Self Directed IRAs are, they're not very good.
2. Big Brokerage houses love Self-Directed IRAs, but hate Solo 401Ks.
3. Big Brokerage houses collect custodial fees on Self-Directed IRAs.
4. 401Ks give us practically everything we need to secure our financial future
5. 401Ks allow us to borrow our own retirement money! (IRAs don't.)
6. We can deduct the interest we pay our own 401K if used for business purposes.
7. There are no deductions for interest with IRAs because borrowing is completely off limits.
8. 401Ks don't incur UBIT as frequently as IRAs! (IRAs incur UBIT a lot, reducing returns.)
9. 401Ks don't incur UDFI. (IRAs incur UDFI on all leveraged transactions, creating a UBIT problem.)

10. 401Ks have no income limits on their Roth or Traditional contributions. (Roth IRAs become unavailable to big earners, TIRAs lose their deductibility.)
11. We establish a small Roth IRA to act as our "Get Out of Jail Free" card.
12. When we transfer to our Roth IRA before age 59 ½, we can access our money penalty free with a 72t distribution.
13. When we transfer to our Roth IRA before age 70, we escape required minimum distributions (RMD).
14. We can distribute property instead of cash to ourselves Tax Free from our R01K.
15. After age 59 ½ we can make short term transactions with no short term capital gains tax imposed.
16. We can invest in precious metals.
17. We can invest in land in foreign countries.
18. We can invest in foreign stocks and set up foreign brokerage accounts.
19. When investing in the R01K, you:
    - Pay No Short Term Capital Gains
    - Pay No Long Term Capital Gains
    - Pay No Unrelated Business Income Tax (if done correctly)
    - Incur no Depreciation Recapture
    - Avoid 1031 Exchanges
    - Pay No Income Tax – Ever
20. We have total control of our retirement and our future.

Please understand that this is the tip of the ice berg, or rather, the crest of the land that makes up Party Island. There are strategies that lie beyond the scope of this book. There are strategies that involve co-investing with your Roth IRA (can't roll it over, remember?), co-investing with your kids' Coverdell Educational Savings Accounts (ESA), your Health Savings Account (HSA) and other people's 401Ks. You can learn how to deduct your kids' Roth from your own earned income. You can deduct your kids' CESA as well. You'll learn how to pay your children so you get a tax deduction for them allowing them to fund a Roth IRA and a Coverdell ESA. You'll learn how to have your kids pay for their piano lessons, hockey equipment, summer camps and whatever else they need, and you'll be able to deduct it all. You'll learn, not only to teach good financial education to your kids, but to instill in them all the principles they need to flourish as adults.

Right now it's up to you. Is there a lot more you need to know to maximize the use of these powerful tools? Absolutely. Is there a mountain of knowledge you need to digest before you jump in and start investing in real estate? Without a doubt. Will you do it? If you're like 95% of Americans, you won't. You'll read this book, marvel at its concepts, put it on your shelf or sell it to Half Price Books. Or you won't have even read it at all.

But if you really want to make a difference in your life and the life of your family, you'll do a few things.

1. You'll find an investor's group in your area and meet with people who are investing in real estate.
2. You'll continue to read. You'll buy the next book in this series. You'll buy a bunch of Robert Kiyosaki's books and books by Ed Slatt and Daniel Solin.
3. You'll cruise the net looking for 401K advice.

4. You'll talk to your friends about this.
5. You'll take action.

As said earlier in this book, knowledge without action is dead: Knowledge plus action is power. My hope is that you, from reading this book, are inspired to power. Party wisely; party powerfully.

ABOUT THE AUTHOR

An autodidact, Michael McDermott developed curricula then taught continuing education for licensed intermediaries in the state of Wisconsin. Partnering with Richard Heaton, together they taught courses on the use of, insurance and related products as they related to Title 19 regulations and retirement plans. The use of insurance products and mutual funds remained his focus until taking some training in the advantages of real estate in these retirement plans.

Using his fundamental knowledge of these plans coupled with his experience in real estate, McDermott developed an educational seminar promoting the advantages of marrying the two together. He soon developed a clientele that achieved extraordinary returns using this knowledge.

Made in the USA
San Bernardino, CA
22 January 2014